When Hope is Enough

Wendy Reese

Wendy Reese

Dedication

My beautiful daughters. Being your mother has been the biggest joy of my life.

I am proud of the woman that you have become. I love that my opinions did not automatically become yours. I love that you are your own person with your very own moral compass.

I love that not only are you my daughters, but also, you are my friends.

I love you both more than you will ever know.

Mom

Table of Contents

Title Page
Dedication
1 A Mother's Worst Nightmare
2 Welcome to the World Baby Ivy
3 The Two Goodbyes
4 The Floor With all the Windows
5 When There is Hope
6 When Hope Becomes Despair
7 Melissa's Miracle
8 The ECMO Circuit
9 The Faces Behind the Mask
10 As One Life is Ending
11 Who Said I Wanted to Die
12 The Countdown
13 Papa
14 Washing Hair
15 Outside
16 Sleeping Meds and Strange Music
17 Visiting Day
18 Going Home
19 Epilogue
20 Acknowledgements

Wendy Reese

When Hope
is Enough

Hope...Such a small word for an immense feeling.

Hope is an ache. A deep yearning for something that you want so badly but it is just out of reach. Hope was the emotion I felt most as I sat next to my daughter in the ICU. Hope is emotion that swelled in my heart making it feel like it would not be able to contain the feeling and might just burst open and the hope would spill out. I hoped so hard for a miracle for Melissa and I guess I must have hoped hard enough.

I don't know if I really believed in miracles before all of this happened, but I guess you don't have to. That's what makes them miracles.

Chapter One

A Mother's Worst Nightmare

"Melissa, close your lips around this and take deep breaths." said the respiratory therapists urgently. Her baby blue scrubs were wrinkled and limp. Little blond tendrils of hair had pulled out of the cloth cap on top of her head, and curled in damp rings around her warn face. I could see the deep, red indentations the mask had left alongside her nose and mouth when the mask readjusted itself on her face when she turned her head. She was exhausted. Her voice held a little frustration, but I could also hear desperation.

Melissa replied in a whispered voice, "I will. I just need a second."

"We have to do this now! There are too many other patients to treat. I don't have a second to give you!" The hospitals were overflowing with patients. Masks, gloves, and ventilators were in short supply and the staff was running on fumes.

"I can't. I just can't," Melissa said in resignation. She sat slumped over in the bed and she was holding the breathing treatment mouthpiece down at her lap. "I'm going to die," she whispered. It was a statement. She didn't even sound afraid, but

I was scared to death. My heart broke watching someone that I loved so much suffer through this.

I was sitting on the edge of the bed. "No, you are not going to die," I said with conviction.

"Mom, I can't." She shook her head from side to side and shrugged one shoulder up as if to say, oh well. She lifted her hand, holding the breathing treatment, and then let it flop back down onto her lap. "I'm done, and I'm going to die."

I could see that Melissa was tired, and that she was giving up. Fear, unlike anything that I have ever experienced in my 55 years, washed over me. "I won't let you give up. Please, please put that back into your mouth," I say, as I push her hand back toward her mouth. "Put this in your mouth and breathe!" I begged, "because the alternative is unacceptable."

Forty-eight hours later, my beautiful, vibrant, sarcastic daughter would be placed on a ventilator.

August 16, 2021

Several days prior to Melissa's hospitalization, I received a call from her. "Mom, Ian has COVID." Ian is Melissa's fiancé, and the father of their 3-year-old daughter Harley.

"Are you sure?" I asked, hoping that she would say she was not sure, and that maybe it was just a cold.

"I'm sure. He took an at-home COVID test, and it turned positive right away. He feels pretty bad."

Ian had isolated himself in the back bedroom, hoping that it was not too late to prevent Melissa, who was 38 weeks pregnant, and their youngest daughter Harley from catching COVID.

Melissa and I decided I would make the two-hour drive to Orlando to help her with Harley and Ian.

Wendy Reese

When I arrived, Melissa was in pajamas. Her long dark hair was up in a messy ponytail, and she was holding a rag and some antibacterial cleaning spray. She had been busy all morning trying to clean all the counters and doorknobs, hoping it might prevent the rest of us from getting ill. Two days later, she tested positive for COVID.

My husband had done some research on pregnancy and COVID. This is how we learned how dangerous the Delta variant was during pregnancy. Our Governor had set up monoclonal antibody stations for people who were at high risk and my husband urged me to take Melissa for treatment.

Melissa already had an appointment to see her OB the next day and she wanted to ask her about the treatment that my husband had suggested. Melissa called the office the next morning to let them know she was COVID positive. The nurse who answered the phone instructed Melissa to come after business hours that day to avoid exposing other patients.

After examining her, the doctor wanted to delay the delivery until the COVID infection was gone.

Melissa came home with the news that the surgery was going to be postponed, and that the doctor said they just needed to let the illness run its course. I asked her what the doctor had said about monoclonal antibodies. She replied she had given the doctor the information, and the doctor was going to investigate it.

August 21, 2021

Melissa was ending the first full week of her illness. She was beginning to feel better, but I was now feeling ill. I knew it had to be COVID. Since Ian and Melissa were both feeling better, and I was still hoping my granddaughter might escape illness, I drove home and sequestered myself in a bedroom so as not to expose the rest of my family. I should have just stayed because I ended up driving back the next day when Melissa's breathing difficulty worsened.

I took her to the ER in Orlando and dropped her off in front of the hospital door. She had to go in alone because security was not letting anyone in but the patient. I watched her walk through the doors and then left to find a spot in the parking garage, where I spent the next 4 hours waiting.

I was feeling horrible. My neck, shoulders, back, and hips ached. I was sweaty and exhausted and could not stop coughing. I could not imagine how Melissa felt, as bad as she was.

As I waited for news from Melissa I scrolled through news on my phone. Everything was about COVID. There had already been so much loss of life from this virus. I did not think it was going to get better anytime soon. A heavy weight settled on my chest knowing that for Melissa, this virus could be really bad.

There were a couple of texts from Melissa while she waited for the doctors to decide what they were going to do with her. A couple of hours later, she called to tell me they were going to release her with medication. I was surprised they were going to send her home, but the hospitals were overrun with patients, and they only kept the ones who they felt were in danger. She came home from the hospital and went to bed, where she stayed for the next 20 hours.

August 22, 2021

Ian and I tried to get Melissa up to walk so fluid would not pool in the back of her lungs, but she was struggling for oxygen by this time and just didn't have the energy. We did everything that we could think of to help Melissa, but nothing worked. Her breathing was becoming shallow, and I didn't know what to do.

Wendy Reese

I was standing at her bedside trying to think of anything that may help, but Melissa got frustrated. With a voice so weak that you could barely hear it, she said, "I need help, but nobody is listening to me." My heart hurt to hear the desperation in her voice.

"Melissa honey, you have to go back to the hospital!" I said, as I hurried toward the bedroom door to have Ian call 911.

We stood by helplessly as the EMTs loaded Melissa onto the gurney. Harley, Melissa and Ian's three-year-old, stood in the corner watching. She didn't approach but stood there with her finger in her mouth. Her long blond curls bounced around her face as her head quickly turned to look at Ian, and then me, for reassurance. I did not want her to be afraid of what was happening, so I tried to reassure her that Mommy was going to the hospital where the doctors could help her. I think I was also trying to reassure myself.

Once the EMTs got Melissa into the elevator, Ian and I took Harley to the balcony. She had panicked and tried to get out the door to go with mommy, but we couldn't let her. We had her wave to Mommy when the gurney became visible in the parking lot, as if this were a normal thing instead of a horrible, frightening situation.

Ian and I still did not realize the gravity of the situation, or maybe we just didn't want to.

Since the hospital would not allow either of us to go in with Melissa unless they admitted her, the EMTs advised us to stay home. We tried to make things normal for Harley as we waited for news. We helped her with the puzzles that she loved to put together, all the while waiting for the phone to ring.

As the realization hit that Melissa would not be coming home soon, we had to decide who was going to go stay with Melissa in the hospital, and who would stay home with Harley and Alexandra.

When Hope is Enough

Alexandra was Melissa's 9-year-old daughter from a previous relationship, who was with her father now, but we knew she would want to come and be with Harley as much as she could. Even though there was a five-year gap between their ages, the two girls were best friends. They slept together in the same twin bed, even though there was one bed for each girl. Alexandra and Harley loved to run around the apartment screaming, while an imaginary dinosaur, whose only desire was to eat them for dinner, chased them.

It was plain to see that Alexandra had learned her caregiving skills from watching mommy. I could hear Melissa in her voice as she spoke to Harley. She had the same gentleness in her voice that Melissa had, as she patiently taught Harley her colors, counting, and the alphabet. Harley worshipped Alexandra.

Melissa eventually texted us to let us know she was waiting for the doctor, and we would hear from her once she knew what the doctors were going to do. It felt like days, but it was only four or five hours when we received the next text from Melissa. "I don't have any definite answers yet, but I'm pretty sure they are keeping me. That's all I know so far."

I texted her back. "Have you seen the high-risk OB yet?"

"For a brief moment, but information is coming in very slowly. I'm too tired to type much. They put me in a labor and delivery room, but that doesn't mean anything. You and Ian need to get a rapid test now and take it. If you or Ian are still positive, they will not let you come in, and I will have to be alone. I'm alright though. I feel too crappy to be scared."

I grabbed my purse, jumped into my car, and got to the drugstore as quickly as I could. There was a box of two tests at the first store I went to. I felt like I had struck gold being able to find the tests without having to go to multiple stores. With the pandemic at an all-time high, the stores were often out of stock. As soon as I got to my car, I ripped open the packaging and took the test right there in the driver's seat. I was anxious as I watched the results window; the pink tint flushed over the white screen, the red control line appeared, and with crushing disappointment, so did the positive line. I was only several days into the illness. Ian was well into his second week, and I could only hope that by some miracle, he would test negative.

As I arrived home, I already had the bag with the last unopened test hooked around my wrist. I put the car in park, threw the door open, and ran into the apartment. Ian was standing by the kitchen counter waiting for me as I came in the door. He looked at me, his head tilted to the side, silently asking what my results had been. I shook my head. "I'm positive. Now let's pray that you are not."

He took the test and thank God his results were negative. We had to wait an agonizing 15 minutes, per the test instructions, to be sure that the results were, in fact, negative.

While we were waiting, we received another text from Melissa. "Please tell me as soon as you get Ian's results." She had said in her earlier text that she felt too ill to be scared, but this last text led me to believe that she was scared, at least a little, and she was alone.

Both Ian and Melissa had hospital bags ready to go. They had been expecting the birth of their baby girl and wanted to be prepared even though Melissa was scheduled for a c-section in a few days. Babies don't care about schedules and could decide to come earlier than anticipated. Ian grabbed both bags and ran out the door. I received a text from him soon after he arrived at the hospital. "I'm with Melissa now."

"How is she?" I asked.

"She's hanging in there. We are waiting to hear from the doctors, but Ivy, will be coming tonight. Ivy is the name that Melissa and Ian had decided on for their second child. Ian is a DC Comics fan and both Harley and Ivy were names from the comic book, *Bat Man*. Harley was named after Harley Quinn and Ivy was Harley Quinn's side kick and best friend in the series, so it was a fitting name for the new baby. The baby's heart rate is up, and Melissa is showing signs of pre-eclampsia." Her blood pressure is high, and Ivy's heart rate is elevated. The doctors don't know if the symptoms are caused by lack of oxygen from COVID or from pre-eclampsia but either way the baby needs to be delivered. He said that the doctors were meeting right now to decide the best course of treatment for Melissa, but first they needed to deliver the baby. Melissa needed medications that were not safe to give while the baby was still inside.

Chapter Two

Welcome to the World Baby Ivy

August 23, 2021

You would think that the answer was obvious, do a cesarean and get Melissa on the medication, but the decision was not easily made. The COVID infection was causing Melissa to cough violently with long bouts that would make her face turn red and tighten her abdominal muscles. Her chest would heave up and down as her body tried to clear her lungs of mucus. If Melissa were to have a coughing fit while the doctor was using the scalpel, he risked cutting an artery in Melissa's abdomen or cutting the baby. Putting Melissa under anesthesia would solve the coughing risk, but the anesthesiologist worried Melissa may not survive being put to sleep.

    It was around 11:15 p.m. that I received a text from Ian. The doctors had decided the risk was too great to put Melissa to sleep for the delivery, so they opted to do an epidural and be ready if she were to cough.

    As they wheeled Melissa into the delivery room, I received another text from Ian. "Melissa wants you to tell Alexandra that she loves her." Melissa feared she would not make it through the surgery, and she wanted her daughter to know how much she loved her. It broke my heart that Melissa was having to fear this outcome.

Ivy was born at 12:21 a.m., on August 23, 2021, a healthy 8 pounds, 11 ounces. Melissa held her for a couple of minutes before going to sleep.

Alexandra's Worries

Daddy told me that Mommy went to the hospital last night because she had COVID. He said Mommy had the baby. I was surprised because I didn't think she was going to be born for a couple more weeks. Then I got scared. I have heard people talking about COVID on tv and we have talked about it in class, so I know a lot of people who get it die. I don't want Mommy to die.

Later that morning, we had hopeful news that Melissa was doing better. She had walked a little and had held Ivy for a few minutes. I spoke with her on FaceTime for just a minute or two and she looked wonderful. Melissa was sitting cross-legged on the bed with the baby cradled in her arm. The nurse had brushed her hair into a high ponytail, and she looked so much better.

Melissa spoke in the cheerful voice that I was so used to hearing. She had the biggest, brightest, most beautiful smile on her face as she looked down at the sleeping baby cradled in her arms. I was sure that the worst was behind us, and that Melissa would be home soon.

Later that afternoon, Ian texted me to tell me that although Melissa had been doing very well that morning, she was having trouble keeping her blood oxygen levels up. As her blood oxygen levels decreased, her respiratory rate increased. The doctor had said that Melissa was on the best medications to treat COVID, and now it was a waiting game.

"Is she doing well, or is she still in danger?" I asked, hoping that she would have magically healed.

"I don't believe she's in danger. The doctor said that she is not out of the woods, but she is holding her own."

I felt helpless not being able to be there to help her.

Ian, ever the proud daddy, told me that Ivy had been sleeping on his chest for the last few hours, and she had been so quiet. He texted me a few pictures of Ivy with her head on his shoulder. Her little cheek pressed into his shoulder, making one side of her mouth and nose push up.

While Ian was in the hospital with Melissa, I stayed at their apartment to take care of Harley. Worry slows down time and the day that stretched before me felt unending. I wanted to sit on the couch with my worry and hide, but I had Harley. She was already a mess without mommy and daddy, so I had no choice but to keep myself together and care for her. She was used to daddy being at work, but he came home every night and was always there for goodnight hugs and kisses. Melissa had been a stay-at-home mom for the last year, so Harley did not know how to be without her. All I could do at this moment was to hope and pray that everything would be ok.

Harley and I watched cartoons on Netflix, put her puzzles together so often that she lost interest in them, and eventually told me she didn't know how to do them anymore. We took a walk to the front of the complex where they had a pretty water fountain surrounded by a stone wall where we could sit. Harley loved to run her fingers through the ripples caused by the falling fountain water. We talked about the clouds and the rocks that she had found on the ground. We played there in the water for a while longer until Harley asked to go home to Mommy and Daddy. It was difficult to explain to Harley that they would not be home for a long time. How do you explain this kind of thing to a three-year-old?

When we arrived back at the apartment, I called my husband to give him an update. I had met Donny in January 2016, and by June 2017, we were married. He had not been around for the girls' earlier years, but he loved them. I gave him an update on Melissa's condition, but it was not good news. He had offered to come and help, but I was adamant that he not come. I did not want him to get COVID.

Donny had been checking in with me several times a day, sometimes with questions, and sometimes just to reassure himself that I was okay. With every text and every phone call, he expressed his desire to come.

By this time, all our family and close friends had heard about Melissa, and my phone was ringing off the hook with questions and concern for her. Everyone wanted to help. There was nothing anyone could do, but I appreciated the texts and calls so much.

In the next several hours, Melissa's condition deteriorated, and she was moved to an ICU room where she would have skilled nurses, doctors, and respiratory therapists caring for her. Her lungs were not getting better and could not process the gas exchange appropriately. Carbon dioxide was building up in her blood.

Ian texted that Melissa had taken two steps to the commode and her oxygen saturation dropped into the high 70s. The nurse told him the drop was normal for COVID, and if her numbers didn't consistently go below 80 and stay there, they were okay.

Unfortunately, her oxygen levels continued to lower down into the 70s, and eventually they stopped improving with rest. Melissa was so short of breath by this time and Ian could not get Melissa to take part in the treatments that might help. Her anxiety had grown as catching her breath became more difficult.

It was at this point that Ian asked if I would come, hoping Melissa might respond differently for me.

August 26, 2021

My daughter was sitting up in bed, her legs stretched out in front of her, as she struggled to breathe. She could not lie down because that made breathing even harder. I watched her sitting in that bed, her head tipping forward or sideways as she fell asleep for just a few seconds before jerking awake when she tipped sideways.

The room was dark, and I could see all the numbers on the monitors. Her heart rate was 165 and her respiratory rate was 64 breaths per minute. Her breathing was shallow and rapid, as if she had just run a race, and she felt as if she could not catch her breath.

Nurses and respiratory therapists were in and out of the room, trying to get her to turn onto her side or her stomach, but she just had a c-section the night before, so being on her stomach was painful. The doctors and nurses had learned that placing a patient on their stomach, a practice called proning, helped oxygen enter into the back of the lungs, filling them more fully. The standard of care was that the nurses would try to get the patient to prone every few hours, but Melissa had not been willing to try it yet. "Eventually, a nurse came in and told Melissa that she had to turn over onto her stomach, hoping that position would allow her lungs to expand more fully. Melissa protested, but the nurse put one hand on Melissa's hip and one on her shoulder and said firmly, "At this point, honey, you don't have a choice. You have to do it." With much effort, Melissa turned to her stomach, but the claustrophobia of not being able to breathe, and the pain of her incision, made it impossible for her to stay there. The nurse told me that proning was what was best, but most patients were so anxious, they could not tolerate the position for long.

I sat at the foot of the hospital bed, alternating between rubbing Melissa's feet, and holding her hands when she reached for me. I tried to prop her body between my knees so that when she fell asleep, she would not tip sideways, but that didn't work very well. There was so little that I could do for her, but I would have crawled into that bed and taken her place if there was any way that I could have.

I would guess that when sitting in the hospital with a child that is not doing well, it is only natural to think about the life that you had with them, and the life that they had with friends and families. I had these warm, fuzzy memories, and as I sat at the foot of Melissa's bed, those memories ran through my head.

At the age of twenty-six, I became pregnant. My father was not happy when I told him the news, but I was overjoyed. I did not know the awesome responsibility that I was about to assume. I didn't think about the fact that worry would become my most frequent visitor, and that I would spend the rest of my life worrying and protecting this child, but my dad knew. What my dad did not tell me was how much I would love this little part of me, and that I would do anything to protect her.

Melissa was an eight-pound, eleven-ounce bundle of joy and pride for me. I loved her with every part of my heart. She had terrible trouble with colic though and never slept at night, so neither did I. She cried all the time unless she was held. I couldn't shower or use the restroom unless I was prepared to hear her heart wrenching screams because her tummy hurt. This continued for the first ten weeks of her life.

We became frequent 3:00 a.m. visitors at the coffee shop down the street. The car ride would almost always calm her down and she would sleep well sitting on top of the table with all the diner sounds in the background.

Wendy Reese

The server told me that if I would put a teaspoon of bourbon in her bottle, she would sleep like a dream. I laughed at that because that was how my grandparents got my mother to sleep during a dinner party that they once had, at the advice of their pediatrician. I was not that desperate, so I left the bourbon out the next time I made her bottle.

As Melissa's first Christmas neared, my mother gave her an early Christmas gift. It was a battery-operated bouncy seat. Melissa loved that seat and would happily sit in it for hours. I loved that seat because I could now take a shower and feel human again without the guilt that she needed me to hold her.

Chapter Three

The Two Goodbyes

August 27, 2021, AM

As I sat helplessly, watching Melissa struggling for every bit of oxygen that her lungs could produce, my mind tried to grasp what was happening. How in the world is it possible that we find ourselves in this desperate situation? I could not stop the thought that Melissa might die. I felt desperation: complete, dark, and utter desperation.

The doctor had already discussed the possibility of having to go on the ventilator with Melissa and Ian before I had arrived, so we were aware of that probability. One nurse who was caring for Melissa at the time kept repeating over and over that Melissa did not want to go on a ventilator, that new moms did not survive COVID once placed on the ventilator. I did not want my daughter to keep hearing this horrifying fact because I knew the ventilator was where she was headed. The last thing I wanted was for her to be put on it, already resigned to dying. I wanted her to fight like hell, like she had never fought before.

Two hours and twenty-two minutes later, Melissa asked to be put on the ventilator.

Wendy Reese

August 27, 2021, 1:22 PM

Being intubated and put on a ventilator would be scary for anyone, and Melissa was not excluded from fear. She questioned the nurses several times, wanting reassurance that she would be asleep and unaware when it happened. The two nurses that were in the room tried to reassure her she would not be aware at the time they inserted the intubation tube. She would be asleep the entire time that she was on the ventilator. She was still scared, but she was also exhausted, so she asked for the doctor to be called.

The nurse left the room, but she returned minutes later with several other hospital personnel and a lot of medication and equipment. They hustled around the room, clearing it of anything that might be in the way. I was left standing against the wall, watching with horror, as they prepared to put Melissa to sleep. It did not feel real. It felt like I was watching a television screen and I could simply turn it off, but there was no button to push.

The doctor came in just a few minutes later to speak with Melissa before sedating her and placing the intubation tube into her trachea. They gave me only seconds to say goodbye to my daughter.

I was crying but trying not to let Melissa see, although I do not think I was very successful. They asked me to leave the room. That was the longest walk that I have ever had to make, even though it was only ten feet to the door. There was an internal struggle that I was now fighting. My instinct was to insist on staying in the room, but I knew that my insistence may very well keep Melissa from getting the care that she so desperately needed. My heart was in pieces. It was heart wrenching to watch her struggle for every breath and then have to walk away. Never in my life did I ever think that I would have to answer my daughter, who had just asked, "Am I going to die?"

I was scared, more scared than I have ever been in my life, and more scared than I could have ever imagined being.

Several nurses and the assistant chaplain met me outside Melissa's hospital room. The chaplain introduced herself and tried to reassure me that Melissa was in excellent hands, but I was not interested in being reassured. I felt angry that someone had called the chaplain without asking me. The chaplain being there was a signal to me that Melissa was not going to survive, and I couldn't handle that thought right now. I knew she was trying to bring me comfort and to distract me, but I also knew what being put on a ventilator meant for Melissa, so there was no comfort to be had. She kept talking to me but all I wanted was to be left alone so that I could concentrate on what was happening to Melissa.

I kept trying to look into the small glass window cut out in the brown hospital room door. I was standing on my tiptoes but could only see the backs of the nurses' heads. I was desperate for a glimpse of Melissa. I just wanted to see her one more time.

The doctor came out of the room ten minutes later, and I thought to myself, this is it. Melissa is now on the ventilator, and she has little chance of coming off. What a horrible and negative thought that was. I was told by several people that I should not think that way, that I needed to be positive. I would have given anything to think positively, but all I could feel was fear, panic, and desperate sadness.

As the doctor stopped in front of the open door, I could see past him and into the room. Melissa was still sitting up in bed, and she had not been intubated. The doctor said that he did not think that Melissa needed to be ventilated just yet, and that she may still recover if given a little more time. My heart started racing and hope built up in my chest. I never thought that hope that big could be physically painful, but it was. The doctor felt that, just as the nurse had stated, going on the ventilator was a last-ditch effort, and he did not think that Melissa was there yet. He mentioned that if they could get her anxiety under control, she may be able to escape the ventilator.

I gratefully rejoined my daughter and sat next to her on the bed. She looked so tired, and she told me she didn't know how much longer she could continue to fight. I hoped and prayed that this reprieve would allow Melissa the time that her lungs needed to heal.

August 27, 2021, 5:00 PM

The nurses continued to come in and out of the room with different treatments. They tried dosing her with narcotics, hoping that they would lower her respiratory rate, but they had little to no effect. They tried beta blockers for her heart rate, but the medication only lowered it a little and lasted for only about twenty minutes before her heart resumed its race.

She went from a small nasal oxygen cannula to a clear plastic mask that covered her nose and mouth, and finally, a positive pressure air mask. The mask fit tightly over her head. The top of it rested on her forehead and completely covered her face. There was a brown tube coming out of the bottom of the mask that connected to the oxygen spout in the wall. The mask reminded me of the oxygen masks that the fighter pilots used to wear while flying the old fighter jets. The pressure of the oxygen that is delivered through the mask is strong, so strong that it made her lips quiver and shake in the stream of air.

The mask was very uncomfortable for her to wear, so she would remove the straps that slipped over the back of her head and simply hold it to her face. I guess that holding it to her face made her feel a little more in control, but she kept falling asleep for just a few seconds, and that was enough time for the mask to slip down her face.

The nurse came in multiple times to fit the mask back on her head, and eventually she said, "Melissa, I promise you cannot hold this mask to your face all night. You will get used to it, but only if you leave it on."

The inability to breathe, the claustrophobic feeling of wearing the mask, and that air being forcefully blown into her nose and mouth, essentially drowning her with a continuous stream of air, was more than she could tolerate, and she refused to wear it. The nurses told me that anxiety was the biggest hurdle for COVID patients.

The evening went on and a shift change took place. I was sitting on the bed, holding Melissa's hand as the door opened. Several nurses rushed into the room, one of whom took my shoulders and pulled me away from Melissa.

She was speaking in a rushed tone as she informed me that Melissa was going to be put on the ventilator, and I was going to have to leave the room. Melissa's eyes widened in surprise, and mine, in shock. She had just been told a few hours ago that they did not want to go this route, but with no discussion with her, the decision was made.

I pulled away from the nurse who had been trying to push me out the door, and asked, "Why now?" Why had they made this decision now, after we had just been told a few hours ago that this was a bad idea? I needed someone to help me understand this new turn of events, so I requested to speak with the new doctor in private. He stepped to the front of the room, closer to the door, so that Melissa could not hear our conversation. I tearfully, and in a panic, told him that the nurse had told Melissa that if she went on the ventilator, she would not come off. My voice had risen in fear, and I was trying not to cry, but could not stop the tears from rolling down my face and into my mask.

The doctor put his hands on my shoulders and gave them a gentle shake. "That is not true! Who told you that?" he asked but did not wait for me to answer. "I can't predict the future, but right now, Melissa needs to go on the ventilator. Her blood gas is getting higher, and when—not if—she goes into respiratory failure, she will have to wait until we can get here. If we are in the middle of working with another patient, it may take a while. We do not want that to happen," he said firmly.

Given the explanation, I guess there really wasn't a choice. I did not want Melissa to end up in respiratory failure and have no help available, so the horrible realization was that this was really going to happen this time.

I walked back to the bed where Melissa was still sitting. She was breathing more rapidly than before. I wanted to wrap my arms around my baby, kiss her booboo, and make it better like I could when she was younger, but this time there was no making things better.

I put the palm of my hand against her cheek and leaned down to kiss her forehead. My voice cracked as I choked the words out of my throat, "You will wake up, and I will be here waiting for you!" Melissa could only nod her head, acknowledging that she had heard me. I stepped away but immediately came back to kiss her again, whispering, "I love you so much!" in her ear.

She mouthed, "I love you too," but no sound came out.

I can't even find the words to describe how difficult it was to force myself to walk away from Melissa. It felt wrong. I had this feeling that somehow, if we were together, that nothing could touch us. I felt physical pain as I moved away from her and backed out of the room. My eyes never left her face, but she was looking down at the bed, trying to catch her breath.

The hospital staff that had filled her room watched as I walked out, waiting for the door to close behind me before exploding into action. This time I was not even trying to hide the tears streaming down my face as the sobs shook my chest. How does a mother walk away from her child knowing that these were probably the last few moments of that child's life? Yet here I was, once again, standing outside the room.

There were several nurses waiting outside the door. Someone handed me a box of tissues, and someone else brought over a chair that I had no interest in sitting in. I was wearing a cardboard N95 mask that pressed tightly to my face, leaving a dent in the bridge of my nose and making it difficult to breathe, especially while crying. A young nurse handed me a pink paper mask and told me I could breathe more easily with the cloth mask.

Once again, I found myself looking into the room through the little window in the door. The Mommy instinct that told me to burst back through the doors and stop this madness was almost irresistible, but I knew that this time I could not fix it. This was not a ghost in the closet or a monster under the bed. This time I could not make it go away.

August 27, 2021, 7:45 PM

I watched as Melissa struggled. Someone moved to the head of the bed and took her head in his hands to hold her still. I placed my palms against the door and got up on my tiptoes, hoping to see over the heads of the nurses. "Why are they holding her down?" I shrieked. "They said that she would be asleep!"

The thought that they would intubate her while she was still awake was horrifying! The nurse put her arm around me and pulled me tightly to her side as she assured me it was normal for her to struggle, even though she was sedated and was not aware. I was not sure that I believed her, thinking she may just be telling me what I wanted to hear. I became even more concerned when the doctor moved away, and I saw my daughter arching forward with her head lifted off the pillow, her chin was raised, and she was moving her head side to side. The intubation tube was protruding out of her mouth.

This will be one of the most vivid and disturbing memories that will haunt me for years to come.

The doctor walked to the door and opened it quickly. He poked his head out and asked me if Melissa used any street drugs.

"No, of course not!" I replied. "Why? What's wrong? Is she still awake? Why is she struggling?" I knew I should stop asking questions and let him answer, but I had lost control, and the questions just spilled out of my mouth.

He reassured me that the medication that had been used to sedate Melissa would prevent her from remembering any of this; however, they were having trouble sedating her enough, and they had, in his words, "given her enough medication to sedate an elephant." Knowing that she wouldn't remember what was happening wasn't really much reassurance. She may not remember later, but did she know now?

They were eventually able to sedate Melissa completely, and the ventilator was now breathing for her. The doctor came out of her room and knelt on the floor in front of the chair I had just sunk into. I was speaking to my mother, trying to explain to her what had just occurred, but between the crying and my brain's inability to process what had just happened, I was failing miserably. The doctor motioned for me to give him the phone. He spent the next ten minutes talking to my crying mother, patiently explaining why Melissa had needed the ventilator. As he spoke with my mother, his hand sat on my knee, which he would occasionally pat in reassurance. The kindness that this doctor showed us on the worst day that we could ever imagine was profound.

After some time, the nurses allowed me back into the room to stand with Melissa. Someone had cut her nightgown off and had replaced it with a blue and white hospital gown. They had cleaned the room, and the nurses were busy charting. I stood there looking at her, thinking over and over, I can't believe this. I just can't believe that this is really happening. That mantra replayed itself over and over in my head. I kept thinking to myself, wake up, please wake up, as if I was in the midst of a nightmare, but it wasn't a nightmare, at least not the kind that I could wake up from.

My mind was stuck between hope and despair; hope because I so desperately wanted to have it, and despair because I understood the reality of the ventilator. My heart was shattering in tiny pieces, and the pain was unbearable.

As I stood next to the bed and looked down at my daughter, I did not see the grown woman that she was. I saw the smart, curious little girl that she had been. She was such a wonderful child, but she was not perfect. Her curiosity would frequently lead her to experiment with things that would ultimately get her, and sometimes me, in trouble.

Melissa was about two years old when my landlord knocked on my apartment door. He calmly explained that as he walked by Melissa's bedroom window, he noticed she was coloring all over one wall with a crayon. I had left her alone for only a couple of minutes, but in that short time, she had drawn what would equate to Michelangelo's Sistine Chapel. She was very proud of her artwork, and I am the one who was guilty of leaving her alone long enough to do it, so how could I get mad?

Fortunately, I was friends with my landlord's wife, so we didn't get into too much trouble. He even came in and helped us clean the marks off the wall.

Shortly after the crayon debacle, Melissa decided to find out what would happen if she balled up toilet paper and shoved those little balls as far up her nose as possible. An emergency room visit is what would happen. After several attempts to reach the offending balls of toilet paper with tweezers, I decided I didn't want to accidentally perform a lobotomy, so we let the professionals retrieve them.

I met Eric, Melissa's stepfather, when I was twenty-nine, and Melissa was three. Eric and I dated for a year before getting engaged. He was willing and able to join a family that was already started, and things were good.

We moved to Jupiter, Florida, from sunny California just one week after getting married. It was very difficult to leave my mom and my brother and sisters, as we were all very close, but this is the way of the world. We grow up and move away to start our new adult lives, even though it is hard.

We had been married for a couple of years before I became pregnant with Melissa's sister, Emily. I was so happy to be having a second child, and Melissa was excited about being a big sister.

Eric and I enrolled Melissa in a big sister class they had at the local hospital. I still remember the picture of Melissa with her little surgical cap and hospital gown that they provided all the children in the class. She was clutching the baby doll to her chest, holding it just like the nurses had taught her to.

When we brought Emily home, Melissa took her job as big sister seriously. I had been a little worried that she might have trouble because she would now need to share my attention. Eric was gone a lot for his job, so Melissa was used to having all of my attention. It was and always had been just Melissa and me most of the time. I did not know how I could love another human being as much as I love her until Emily came along. I loved them both so much, but differently. They had very different personalities and needed to be loved and cared for differently. Melissa did not have any trouble sharing me. In fact, she happily accepted Emily into our little family and was always there to help make bottles, bring me diapers and wipes, and eventually learned how to change diapers by herself.

As Emily, our beautiful little redheaded girl grew, she would seek Melissa out. When Melissa came into the room, Emily would always crawl over to her. Melissa was very patient and would allow Emily to climb onto her back and play with her hair, even though Emily pulled on it.

Melissa was about nine when she came home with the dreaded chickenpox. The school sent her home with a few little spots on her face, but as I undressed her, I found them covering her trunk. She was running a slight fever and was just not feeling very well. It wasn't long before I found the spots on Emily too.

We spent the next three or four nights camped out on the living room floor. The girls were very uncomfortable with the itching, but we made the best of things and treated the three nights as a camp-out. Melissa and I took turns telling scary stories. We read books and played some board games. It was easier for me to care for them if they were together in the same room and I didn't want to keep Eric up all night because he was on call and may have had to go to work. He was a commercial pilot and was on call a good majority of the time.

When Melissa was 12 and Emily was 5, Eric and I separated and then divorced. Regretfully we had forgotten how to communicate effectively so we ended the marriage, but not the friendship. We worked together and continue to stay friends, and I am forever grateful that we did not become like other divorced couples who end up hating each other. Once again, it became just the girls and me.

I rented a townhome not too far from where we had lived in Jupiter Farms, a little community on the east coast of Florida. Melissa started middle school where she met the four girls that would become her lifelong friends and one boy who would become the father of her daughter Alexandra.

We had so many memories, the three of us. So many first days of school and Tooth Fairy visits, so many birthdays and Christmases. I remembered how the girls would always sneak out into the living room, Melissa holding Emily's hand, helping her look but not touch, and peek at what Santa had left for them. I allowed it because that is what my brother, sisters, and I had done as children. It was part of the fun.

We lived happily in the townhome for a little over a year until I purchased our very own home about forty-five miles north of Jupiter. Melissa was not excited to leave her friends and Kevin. I understood the move was going to be difficult for both Melissa and Emily, but the mortgage would be much less than rent.

Now, as I stood there watching the nurses preparing Melissa to be transferred by ambulance to the hospital across the street, those memories seemed so far away.

At the urging of the nurses, I went home for the night. I just didn't know if I had the strength to watch Melissa being moved, and I was afraid that I would be in the way.

It was nearing midnight as I made my way down the street and into the parking garage. I walked mindlessly to my car, feeling emotionally numb. My brain was whirling with thoughts of how I was going to tell Alexandra. How would I tell her about Mommy without lying, while still giving her the ability to be hopeful? How would Harley react when Mommy does not come home? How would I go on if Melissa did not survive? It would forever change all our lives, and none of us would ever feel whole again.

My husband had driven from Port Saint Lucie earlier in the evening, after being told that they had put Melissa on the ventilator. I told him when I called that there really wasn't anything that he could do, and that I would be home late and up early, but he couldn't stand the thought of me being alone that night. His support meant everything to me and gave me strength. I was so tired by the time that I got back to the apartment that we didn't even watch TV or talk. He set out the air mattress that I had been sleeping on and then put me to bed and tucked me in. He made a bed on the couch for himself. I was grateful that he had not listened to me and had come, even though I told him he didn't have to. I really needed him.

Alexandra's Worries

I talked to Daddy, and he told me that Mommy was really sick, and she needed a machine to breathe for her. I know they put a tube down your throat when you are on a ventilator and I'm afraid mommy can feel it, even though Daddy and Grammy said she can't. What if she can?

Chapter Four

The Floors with all the Windows

August 28, 2021

Melissa and Ian's newborn was being cared for in the hospital nursery while Melissa was in the hospital. Neither Ian nor I knew what was going to happen, and we felt the nurses would be able to meet Ivy's needs better than we could for the moment. The nurses would send us updates about how much she was sleeping, how much she was drinking (a lot!), and that they were holding and rocking her often.

Once Melissa was transferred to the hospital across the street, Ian wanted Ivy to come home. We both drove separately, Ian with Harley, and me in my car so that I could stay with Melissa for the rest of the day. I sat with Harley in the car while Ian went in to pick up Ivy.

Watching Ian head inside to pick up Ivy reminded me of the day that Melissa brought Alexandra home. She and Kevin were so young, but they were dedicated to keeping Alexandra clean, safe, and well fed. They took turns holding her, and I had to beg to have a turn. They had initially come home with me and stayed for the first week. Melissa was nervous about keeping this tiny human alive and she felt more comfortable with me helping her.

Sadly, after the first week, they headed home to stay with Kevin and his parents. I missed them being with Emily and me, but Kevin's parents had more room, so they were the obvious choice.

Melissa came to visit often so I felt lucky that I could form such a close bond with Alexandra. I loved seeing the joy on Melissa's face as Alex grew and started to walk and talk. Melissa took countless videos of Alexandra and would try to get her to say or do something that had tickled her. She particularly thought that the way Alexandra said balloon and bath was the cutest thing she had ever heard. Alexandra would excitedly exclaim "badooch!" every time that she went to the Publix grocery store and saw the colorful balloons at the checkout stand and would insist on taking a "batch" every night so that she could play with her water toys.

She, just like her mother when she was little, would get such a kick out of foaming up her long dark brown hair and coiling it up on the top of her head like a Santa hat. That was made even better when we used the soap foam to create a white pointy beard on her little chin.

As Ian left the hospital, carefully carrying little baby Ivy, who looked exactly like her mom when she was a baby, I was happy that he had wrapped Ivy in the linen Disney "Up" scarf that Melissa had been so excited to bring her home in. The nurses had dressed Ivy in a purple tie died onesie, and Ian had topped it all off with a big white bow on the top of Ivy's head.

As Ian placed the car seat, with the screaming baby, into the car, Harley looked at us in confusion. "Baby's crynen." That was her word for crying. She didn't sound as if she was really sure about putting this screaming baby into the car and allowing her to move into the fairly quiet home that she was so used to, but I knew that she and her big sister Alexandra, would come to love Ivy with an endless bond.

Ian, Harley, and Ivy headed for home while I walked across the street to the hospital where Melissa had been transferred. As I walked down the hall toward Melissa's new room, I stopped to check in with the nurse at the nurse's station.

While I was standing there, one nurse that had been sitting at a charting desk next to me stood up and wrapped her arms around me. We stood like that for several seconds before she let go and sat back down. She didn't say a word, but she didn't have to. I could walk right past this nurse on the street, and I would never recognize her. She was dressed in a yellow paper gown with white cuffs that fit tightly at the wrist. The paper belt wrapped around her waist twice because she was so little. Her hair was covered with a nylon hair net, and she was wearing a pink paper mask as well as a face shield. I don't need to remember what she looked like because I will remember her heart, and on this day, at this moment, she gave me a little piece of it. I will never forget her.

Before I was allowed into the room, the nurse took me to a small cart that was sitting against a wall. The cart contained all that I would need to be as protected as possible from the virus. The same yellow paper gown that the nurses were wearing, a hairnet, two gloves on each hand because one was not enough, a hard cardboard N95 mask, and a face shield that fogged up as I breathed.

The room was situated right across the hall from the nurse's station, so I could see right into Melissa's room. Instead of a solid wall, there was a large window with a curtain that could be drawn for privacy. It was big and bright for a hospital room, with clean painted gray walls and a long bench covered with blue vinyl. Toward the back of the room was a big, uncovered picture window, and just outside of the window was a rooftop helicopter pad.

Melissa was lying on her back in a bed that was in the right corner of the room. Someone had covered her with a blue hospital blanket. Ventilator tubes were coming up out of her throat and mouth, and were clipped to plastic hooks, attached to silver movable arms. The arms were connected to a blue ventilator that made a sucking sound and then a whoosh as it pulled the air from her lungs.

All I could do was stand at the entrance to the door and look in with shock. I was overwhelmed seeing my baby's body, swollen and bloated. Her feet were so filled with fluid that they appeared to be square blocks instead of feet with toes. Her chin and neck looked extended from the tube that had been inserted into her lungs to breathe for her. The intubation tube had two pieces of white medical tape that wrapped around the base of the tube and then pulled to either side of her cheeks to secure it to her face.

The most shocking thing was how still Melissa was except for the rise of her abdomen as air was forced into her lungs, followed by an abrupt drop, as the air was pulled back out.

This was the first of nine days that Melissa would spend in this room.

Once I regained my composure, I made my way over to the bed and leaned down to kiss Melissa. All I could reach without fear of dislodging anything was her forehead. I stood over the bed for a few hours stroking the hair back from her forehead, alternating between calmness and crying.

Someone had taken the messy, tangled bun out of Melissa's hair, brushed it, and it now lay in a neat braid that came across her left shoulder. They had put soft music on in the background. These simple gestures meant the world to me; it meant that the people taking care of my child cared.

Nurses would bustle in and out every thirty or forty minutes to do something. I noticed that every time anyone was going to touch or move Melissa, they always told her what they were going to do, even though they did not know if she could hear them. I could tell that they were used to speaking to the patients, and not doing it just because I was there. That made me feel good. It made me feel like they viewed Melissa as a person instead of just a body in that bed.

One nurse noticed that I had been standing, so she pointed out the wooden folding chair that was hanging on a wall by the door. I could have sat on the bench with the cushion, but I would not have been close enough to Melissa to touch her. I set the chair as close to the bed as I could get it and sat down to hold Melissa's hand because there was nothing else that I could do.

When the nurse came back into the room, I asked, "Do you think she can hear me?"

"We really don't know," she said gently. "Keep talking to her. If she can hear you, your voice will be familiar and help her feel safe."

I have heard from nurses before that they really don't know what people can hear when they are in a coma and heavily sedated. Some people report they remember absolutely nothing while others can repeat conversations word for word. If there was even the slightest chance that she would have the smallest snippet of memory, I wanted her to know that I was there, so I just talked. I told her how much I loved her, and that a huge part of me would go with her if she did not come back to us.

I told her that her little sister Emily needed her because she could tell Melissa things that she may not want to tell me. Melissa was Emily's confidant. She could talk to Melissa about periods and boys and didn't feel that she had to be careful with her questions. I would have happily answered them, but I am Mom and Melissa was easier to talk to.

I told her that Alexandra, Harley, and Ivy needed her. Who would talk to Alexandra about growing up and becoming a young lady? She was only nine years old, and she needed her mom. Alexandra already had a very hard time because she was not always with Melissa. She would go between her mom and dad's houses, and although she loves both of them, there are some things that girls need to talk to mom about, because dad just will not do.

Who would translate what Harley was saying? She was four years old and clearly had a lot to say, but sometimes her brain was faster than her tongue, and the words would come out jumbled. Melissa almost always knew what she was saying. Who would sit on the floor and rock Harley when she fell off the bed, doing something that she shouldn't, and bloodied her lip?

What would it be like for Ivy if she had to grow up never knowing her mommy? Melissa would never get to see her first smile, her first steps, or her first day of school.

I could not stand the thought that Melissa would not be here to do and see these things. The girls needed to touch and feel, hear, and see Melissa, not remember her from a photograph. I needed that too.

I told her that Ian needed his partner in life. He needed help to raise the two precious, beautiful children that had been placed in their care. He needed the one person who got him. Melissa has a bad habit of saying "your face…" to everything Ian would say. He would say, "The kitchen is messy." She would reply, "Your face is messy." He would say, "This song is so stupid," and she would reply, "Your face is stupid." It annoyed Ian to no end, and that is why she always said it. It would irritate Ian, but it would also make him laugh. They had this wonderful relationship, with clever banter and so much affection. I could not imagine life without witnessing this beautiful relationship continue to change and grow as the years passed.

A few hours after my arrival, the doctor, dressed in the same isolation gear, poked his head in the door and asked to speak with me outside the room. I set Melissa's hand gently at her side, "I'll be right back, sweetheart. I just need to talk to the doctor." I walked out of the room into the hallway.

The doctor was young, very tall, and had dark hair and skin. The doctor helped me untie the paper belt around my waist and dispose of it. He did not sugarcoat the seriousness of the situation. "Melissa is very sick, and her lungs are badly scarred." He explained to me that COVID causes deep scarring in the lungs, and that scar tissue gets very ridged, preventing the lungs from expanding. "She has a fever, but we have started her on antibiotics that will hopefully help."

"Is Melissa going to live?" I asked, desperately wanting him to say "of course" but he did not.

"We just don't know right now. The ventilator is doing the work of breathing for her and we hope her lungs will improve with rest."

"But what is your best guess?" I pressed.

He then explained that there was no treatment at this point. All they could do was to use everything at their disposal to keep Melissa alive long enough to give her lungs time to heal. There were no guarantees that they would heal, and if they did, there were no guarantees that they could wean her off the ventilator.

"Are her chances 50/50, better, or worse than that?" I persisted with my questioning.

"I won't give odds anymore because I have been disappointed too many times." He was staring into the window of the room watching the numbers on the ventilator screen. "She is very young," he said thoughtfully and almost to himself. "I promise we are going to do everything that we can to help her."

I would ask this question again and again for the next couple of days, each time hoping for a different answer, but each

When Hope is Enough

doctor would give me the same answer. The nurses, however, were a little more forthcoming, and almost all of them said, in one way or another, that they did not expect Melissa to survive, but that we should continue to hope.

Chapter Five

When There is Hope

August 30, 2021

On this day, I would leave with a little more hope. I came in early and sat with Melissa until the doctor's rounds ended. While I was waiting for her doctor, I played some videos that Alexandra, Ian, and Melissa's dad, Eric, had recorded for her. We were not sure if Melissa could hear, but if she could, we wanted her to hear the voices of the people that loved her the most.

Yesterday, before I left, I had asked the nurse if it was okay to bring lotion in so that I could massage Melissa's legs and feet. Melissa had wanted me to rub her legs before they placed her on the ventilator, so I thought that it may bring her some comfort now. The nurse said that it would be fine to bring the lotion and that massaging her legs might help with some of the swelling.

I stood at the end of the bed for an hour each morning and each evening massaging Melissa's legs and feet. I would move all her joints, toes, ankles, knees, and hips before moving on to each arm. The hospital policy was that range of motion (moving each joint through its complete range of motion) was not provided for patients while on the ventilator. I'm sure that they simply did not have enough personnel, so I did it myself.

As I stood at the end of the bed rubbing Melissa's legs, I noticed nurses looking in through the glass door. I knew what they were thinking, and it made me sad. They were looking in the little window with sympathy. They thought Melissa would not survive, and that what I was doing was unnecessary. For me, it was an absolute necessity. I couldn't do much for Melissa. This was a battle that she had to fight and win herself, but it gave me the feeling that I was doing something that might be of benefit to her, even if only a little.

While I was speaking with the doctor later in the afternoon, he reported Melissa was doing very well. They had lowered her ventilator setting to sixty percent, which was very encouraging. When she was first put on the ventilator, she was at one hundred percent support, but at this moment, her lungs were doing some of the work instead of relying fully on the ventilator. I asked him, as I did every day, "What are her chances of recovering?" but today he did not say that he would not guess.

"I am very hopeful." The words that I had been most wanting to hear had just come out of his mouth. This must be a good sign, I excitedly thought to myself! He had been refusing to make a prediction, and now he was saying he was hopeful. Hope is a beautiful thing but it can be a very slippery slope. Everything was looking up, and I was so incredibly relieved. When I left that evening, I felt like I was walking on air! I felt so light, like an enormous weight had been lifted from my shoulders. I called my mom, like I did every evening as I walked through the dark parking garage, to give her a report for the day.

My mother had been such a support for me. She allowed me to call, and I could be an emotional mess. I did not have to guard my emotions when I spoke with her. She did not tell me how I should feel or what I should do. She just listened and made supportive sounds as I spoke. I know it was hard on her listening to my pain because she had her own pain when thinking about Melissa, but she did it anyway. She could always talk, and she took the burden of calling all the family members with updates so that I did not have to. I loved all the messages from family and friends but didn't always have the strength, or the words, to answer them. I was just too emotionally raw.

I had pretty much moved into Melissa's apartment with Ian and the girls since my home was two hours south of where the hospital was. Ian had made me feel welcome and never made me feel as if I was intruding. That evening I walked through the front door and saw little baby Ivy in her swing. I just couldn't resist picking her up and snuggling with her, even though it woke her. She was soft and warm and smelled like Downy. When I held her in my arms, I felt like I was holding a little part of Melissa, and I guess I was. As I looked down at Ivy's face, her little mouth making tiny sucking motions, I thought to myself, how is it possible to feel joy and sorrow at the same time?

I felt the awful weight of guilt; holding this little baby in my arms brought me joy. How could I dare to feel any happiness at all when Melissa could not hold this child that she nurtured in her body for nine months? I wondered if Melissa would feel cheated when she woke up and realized that she had missed the first few weeks of her child's life?

As I rocked Ivy, I remembered the complete and utter love that I had felt when I held both of my newborn daughters and my heart ached for Melissa that she was not here, sitting in the rocker instead of me. The joy I felt watching Melissa love and care for Alexandra, and then Harley, was a very poignant memory for me.

I thought about the day that she told me that, at sixteen, she was pregnant. She had asked if we could sit down and talk about something. I could tell that whatever she had to tell me must be big, because I could see that she was very nervous. She didn't waste any time and just quickly told me she was several weeks pregnant. I remember feeling scared for Melissa and scared for Kevin, who were now going to be parents before they had even graduated high school. Raising a child is hard work, and it changes your life profoundly. Being a parent is hard even when you feel ready for it. She and Kevin were only sixteen and had not even begun to live.

As the weeks passed, Melissa started having horrible morning sickness, so sick in fact, that the doctor suggested having a nurse come out with IV nutrition because Melissa could not eat or drink anything. The high school was wonderful and provided so much support. I would get calls from the guidance counselor, asking how Melissa was doing. She had set up a system where teachers would bring homework up to the office and leave it in a bin for me to pick up and bring to Melissa, but unfortunately, she was so sick that she never touched any of it.

I remembered how my chest had filled with pride that despite being pregnant, and despite the fierce morning sickness, she finished her junior year of high school online. Soon after giving birth, she finished and graduated high school on time and with her friends, and on the dean's list.

When I took her and her girlfriends to a local park to take graduation photos, Melissa insisted she hold Alex in every one of the pictures that did not include the other four girls. Somewhere along the photoshoot, Alexandra had lost a shoe so you could see one little black shoe and one little bare foot with tiny little chubby baby toes. Melissa thought that the missing shoe made the pictures even more sweet.

Melissa turned seventeen one month after Alexandra was born. As her girlfriends were attending prom, Melissa and Kevin were changing diapers. Neither of them moaned or complained about missing prom or homecoming. Melissa didn't resent that she missed parties or going out, and she didn't expect me to parent Alexandra. She was her mother, and she wanted to care for her herself. She had always been one to do things for herself. I can't recall how many times I heard Melissa's little toddler voice say, "I do it, Mommy." As Melissa grew and her challenges became bigger and much harder, her "I do it" mentality became stronger, and her determination to figure out how to accomplish things you would think that she couldn't was impressive.

She was much older when she became pregnant with Harley but was still plagued with the same horrible morning sickness. The morning sickness confined her to the couch or her bed for several months until it subsided. I was in attendance when Harley was born, and I was in awe of Melissa's strength and composure as her labor intensified. Ian and I left the room while the doctor placed Melissa's epidural, but we received a phone call from her nurse asking us to return to the room as quickly as we could. I did not know how advanced Melissa's labor was because she was so calm and collected. I had begged for that epidural long before I got to that point in my labor with her sister. Shortly after we returned to her room, Harley entered the world.

When she became pregnant with Ivy, she again spent the first several months in bed or on the couch. Melissa and Ian both knew that Ivy would be their last baby. Melissa suffered so much with all three of her pregnancies and I don't think she wanted to do it a fourth time.

Although Melissa and Ian were very excited about Ivy's arrival, Alexandra was not too sure about having a new sibling, and Harley was too young to really understand what was happening. They prepared a space for Ivy's crib. Melissa and I had gone shopping for a changing table and, although she wanted to put it together right away because she was excited, she left it for Ian. There was not much that he could do to take part in the pregnancy, and he just wanted to be involved. Building the baby equipment was a perfect way to involve him.

My girlfriend Jina had sent a few packages of diapers through Amazon and Melissa videotaped Harley opening the box. Melissa was so tickled that Harley got so excited as she pulled the packages out of the box, yelling, "Yay, diapers!" It didn't matter what was in the packages, she was just excited to open them.

Just two weeks before Melissa went to the hospital, we were happily sitting on the bed admiring all the baby gifts. How quickly our entire world had changed with the passage of just a few days.

We were all blissfully unaware as we prepared for Ivy's arrival that our happy little world was about to come crashing down.

August 31, 2021

I had been spending ten to twelve hours a day sitting in Melissa's room and there was a lot of time that I didn't know how to fill. It was impossible to keep a one-sided conversation up for hours, so sometimes I would put Melissa's favorite show, *Gilmore Girls*, on my phone and place it on the pillow by her ear. Sometimes I would read to her. I had really enjoyed reading *Escaping the Giant Wave* by Peg Kehret, so I sat in the chair and read it to Melissa. Sometimes, I would just sit quietly and watch the numbers on her ventilator, willing them to move up or down in the direction that I wanted them to go. Other times, I would just sit and listen to the ventilator keeping Melissa's body fed with oxygen and watch the life flight helicopters that would frequently land, drop a patient off, and then take off again to rescue someone else in need.

Wendy Reese

How strange it was, I thought to myself, that when someone is on a ventilator on a TV show, everything always looks so peaceful. The loved one is sitting by the bed, and the room is silent, but this is fiction and so far from the truth. There is no silence. The room is filled with the whoosh whoosh of the ventilator and the nurses are talking or laughing outside the room. The IV machine is alarming with a beep, beep, beep, and the ventilator is constantly alarming with a higher-pitched beep and then a lower beep. Every time I hear an alarm, my heart drops. Every alarm signaled disaster.

My head was full of thoughts that did not really suit the moment. Melissa would be twenty-eight in thirty-eight days. Will all the people that love her be able to celebrate the day of her birth with her, or would we all be mourning her death? What about Christmas? Christmas would never be the same, and I worried about how her children would react. What would I do with the gifts that I had already purchased?

I thought about the blue flute that was in a plastic storage container in my attic at home. Melissa had been a flute player in the band since middle school, and one year she had found this shiny metallic blue flute advertised online and she wanted it so badly. She talked about it so much that I ended up ordering it and giving it to her for Christmas.

I would have to climb up into the attic and dig it out of the box so I could hopefully give it back to Melissa.

These were such mundane things to think about, but I think my brain knew that my heart was not capable of emotional thought at the moment, so it kept me busy with technical thoughts.

Chapter Six

When Hope Becomes Despair

September 2, 2021

I arrived on the sixth morning excited about the new improvements that I was sure to find, only to notice that her ventilator settings were back up to one hundred percent. Melissa was undressed and covered with a foil blanket that was attached to a small machine hooked to the foot of the bed. The machine was blowing cold air into the foil blanket. Its purpose was to lower Melissa's temperature that had spiked overnight. It looked to me like it was just one more thing that would be miserable if Melissa had any awareness at all.

    I was heartbroken at the backward movement, and my dread came back with a vengeance. I asked today's doctor, as I always did, how he felt Melissa was doing. I knew before I asked that I would not like the answer. "Melissa has a secondary infection, and she is critically ill. She really needs an ECMO machine."

    I had never heard of an ECMO machine before and had no idea what it did or why it was important. For a very brief second, I had a flash of hope. The doctor's next words dashed my hope into the ground. "She needs the machine, but we can't find her one. Our hospital does not have any that are not already in use. We have called other hospitals, but they don't have enough for their own patients." There was frustration in his voice, and I knew it was devastating for the doctors and nurses to lose patients when there was one more thing that may have helped.

The ECMO (*extracorporeal membrane oxygenation) machine is a life support system that has commonly been used for children and adults with either heart and or lung failure. Its original purpose was to keep someone alive while they are waiting for an organ transplant. In Melissa's case, her lungs were so stiffened by the scar tissue from the COVID infection that they could not expand to allow oxygen to enter the parts of her lungs that processed the exchange of oxygen and carbon dioxide. The ventilator was no longer working well enough to blow off the carbon dioxide, which was now building up in her blood, causing her heart rate to increase.

I did not want to accept that we could not get Melissa the machine that she needed to stay alive. How is it possible that we do not have enough machines to treat the people who are dying without one?

When COVID first started there was a fear that we would not have enough ventilators, so our government had companies build more. Why were they not doing that now with this machine?

I questioned the doctor about other locations. "What about New York or California? Why can't we transfer her to another hospital that has one?"

He put his hand on my back and leaned closer to me. "No one has any that are available, and even if they did, Melissa would not survive the trip." I now understood why he did not want to predict survival, as it leaves a bitter disappointment when expectation does not meet reality. But nevertheless, that little voice of hope in my head told me that everything would be okay.

After sitting with Melissa for a while, I left the floor and went outside to the atrium, where I called Ian to let him know about Melissa's decline. I had to steal myself to make the rest of my calls to all the people who had texted and called daily.

When I called my girlfriend Jina, who had provided unlimited emotional support, she immediately got online and asked the people in her prayer circle to pray for an ECMO machine. These people had been praying all along, so many people had, but now... now there was something specific to pray for.

Jina has been my friend since Melissa's first day of kindergarten. Jina's daughter was the same age as Melissa, and they were in the same class. I had just come home from the hospital after having Emily and she and I went to the school to pick Melissa up after her first day of kindergarten. I saw several of the mothers sitting on the wooden rail of a redwood planter box in front of Emily's classroom. Jina was one of them. There were seven or eight of these square redwood planter boxes in the quad, but this one, with its little Charlie Brown tree in the middle, became our bench for the next three or four years. We started a conversation, and that was the beginning of a wonderful friendship.

As we watched our girls grow up, we became fast, snake-rescuing friends, and spent our days together. We lived out in Jupiter Farms, a very rural area of Jupiter, and both our husbands were away a lot for work. We were both very adept at figuring out how to fix things that broke or solving problems that would normally fall to the husbands, but ours were not there.

Jina called me one day, sounding a little perplexed. She had gone out to her back deck and found that a snake had somehow gotten its head and part of its body up through the slats of wood and gotten stuck. I drove over to help.

When I arrived, we both walked out to see the poor thing in its terrible predicament.

We did not want to kill the snake, so we set about figuring out how to release it without causing it harm. We tried to unscrew the two boards, but we had to get the screwdriver too close to its mouth and it kept trying to bite us. With a lot of laughing and a little screeching, we put a small bucket over the head of the snake so it couldn't bite us and pried two boards apart wide enough to allow the snake to fall to the ground below and slither away.

We had been friends for so long that I couldn't really remember a time that I didn't know her.

We talked for several minutes before hanging up and I headed back up to Melissa's bedside.

I left late that afternoon an emotional mess. My granddaughter Alexandra called me on FaceTime as I walked back through the high-rise parking garage to find my car. She was telling me about her day and then, boom, she asked me the question that I had been dreading for Melissa's entire hospitalization. "Is Mommy going to die?" she asked in a small voice. I did not know how to answer her.

"Honey, we just don't know. Mommy is really strong, and she is fighting so hard to stay with us, but she is also really, really sick. The doctors are doing everything they can to help Mommy." My throat had gone dry, and the buzzing in my head made it hard to think.

As I spoke, I held back my tears. I wanted to give her age-appropriate information, not wanting to scare her but also wanting her to be prepared because things were not looking good. While I was on the phone with Alexandra, I was walking around the parking garage trying to find my car. I walked up and down the five story ramp several times and probably passed my car more than once, but nothing was registering in my head. I walked between the cars and around them, but nothing looked familiar. I don't think I was really even seeing the cars as I passed them. I was a body on auto pilot.

I ended the call with Alexandra, but by this time, my grief had taken over, and I could not keep it in check. Grief is a fickle emotion. Sometimes it is a wave gently lapping at my feet. Other times, like now, it is a giant frothing wave crashing over my head. Its fingers wrapped around my ankles and pulled me into the dark murkiness of the sea. Right now, the waves of grief were so powerful that it took my breath away.

I called my husband, and before we had ended the call, he was in the car on the way to Orlando. I was now standing in the middle of a parking garage all alone.

I called my mother who answered right away, as she always did, hoping for news of Melissa.

"Hi," she said, "How is Melissa doing?"

I burst out in hysterical tears, my breath coming in fast, high-pitched sobs. My poor mother, not knowing what I was sobbing about, but fearing that Melissa had died, questioned me as her voice teared up. I was able to tell her that Melissa was still with us, but that she was not doing well. I couldn't get much else to come out of my mouth other than the high pitch sobs that I could not stop.

Never in my wildest dreams could I imagine I would ever have a panic attack, but that was indeed what was happening.

I choked out, "I can't find my car," which just made things worse for my mother. I was breathing so quickly that I was dizzy. I kept telling myself I needed to control my breathing and slow it down. While I was telling myself what to do, I could regain control but as soon as I stopped, it would start all over again. I knew how upsetting this must be for my mother to hear. I know she would have given anything to be there with me and had offered to fly from Washington State, but I had told her there really wasn't anything she could do until Melissa came home.

"What do you mean you can't find your car? Where are you?" She asked, her voice rising in her concern for my state of mind. I guess my brother had been listening to this exchange between my mother and me and asked to take the phone.

"Wendy, what is going on?" he asked.

"I don't think she is going to make it, and I can't find my car!"

Hearing in my voice that I had completely lost control of myself and needed help to calm down, he said, "Wendy, you do not know that Melissa is going to die." His voice was low and firm but reassuring at the same time. "She is having a bad day, but she has had them before."

My brother Scott and I had always been close. We had times when we grew apart and went on with our lives, but we always came back together. I had gotten lucky with my brother growing up. While my friend's brothers were desperately trying to get away from their sisters, my brother was trying to get me to do things with him. He would ask me to go for hikes, or to go bike riding with him. Now, as an adult, I regret all the times I had told him no.

Scott stayed on the phone with me until I found my car and had calmed down. Today, my brother was my hero.

Alexandra's Worries

I called Grammy today. She was leaving the hospital and was trying to find her car. I asked her if Mommy was going to die. I wanted her to tell me the truth, but at the same time, I was afraid of the truth. She said she didn't know. She said Mommy was fighting really hard, but she was really sick, so she couldn't give me an answer.

Chapter Seven

Melissa's Miracle

September 3, 2021

My brother had been right, and the next morning Melissa was doing better. The doctor told me that the decline had stopped, and that she was holding her own. He assured me they were giving her everything they had because she was so young, although I am certain that all patients were given the same treatment. The doctors on the ECMO unit are trying to wean someone off one of the machines, but they just don't know if she will be ready to come off before it was too late for Melissa.

    He did not tell me at the time that there were multiple people at that hospital, as well as many from the hospital across the street, and the nation, who needed that same machine. If this one machine became available, they would have to choose who would live and who would die. What a horrible decision to have to make. There is a very complicated math algorithm that is used to determine which patient has the best odds of survival, so the decision is not made by emotions, but still a horrible decision, nonetheless.

As I sat by Melissa's bed, my mind flipped through memories like the pages of a book. I remembered the time when Melissa wasn't more than 3 years old when she offered me her only dollar. She had overheard a conversation that I had on the phone and thought that it was about money. She was holding the dollar bill behind her back, before presenting it to me in her outstretched little hands, telling me that I could have it because she didn't need it. I remember the picture that I had of her sitting on her knees on my kitchen floor, with her arm stuck deep inside a pumpkin, clearing it of all the pumpkin gunk. I could picture her on the Cracker Barrel porch, sitting in the double rocking chair with her dad. Her little legs barely touched the ground as she pumped them to make the chair rock. "Hey dad, it's like exercising and resting at the same time."

I remembered her first day of school, and I remembered that her teachers would send notes home for the next six years to report that she was talking during class.

I thought about the time that we drove past a pasture full of cows and she got so excited that she ended up excitedly yelling, "Look! Kitties!" She quickly realized her mistake and corrected herself, but it was too late. It became the family joke, and to this day, I still say, "Look at all those Kitties," every time we pass a field of cows.

I remembered all the times that she would call me to tell me something or to just check in. How I loved to hear her voice on the other end of the phone, "Hi Momma!"

Would memories be all that I had left?

September 5, 2021

I arrived this morning, the 9th day, and was met at the door by one of the nurses. I looked in the big window that separated her room from the hallway and noticed that there were several doctors and nurses in the room. The nurses that met me at the door asked me to dress in the isolation gear as fast as I could. Melissa was dying. Her heart rate had risen to a point that her body would not be able to sustain life. She had minutes to a couple of hours before her heart just got too tired and stopped.

I stood there, my feet rooted to the floor, as she somehow managed to dress me. My brain could not comprehend what she was saying. There was just no way for me to understand that I was going to have to exist in a world without Melissa. Somehow, without any conscious thought, my feet propelled me into the room and over to Melissa. I found myself standing beside her. I took her hand in mine and bowed my head, placing her hand against my cheek and I prayed. I prayed, I pleaded, I bargained, and I yelled. There was complete and utter heartbreak as the realization washed over me, that I would outlive one of my daughters. Moms are not supposed to outlive their children. The realization took my breath away.

I called Ian as I sat holding Melissa's hand and told him that he needed to come to the hospital right away. My next call was to my husband, who jumped in the car, wanting to be here for me during this nightmare.

My youngest daughter Emily was at work and was not answering her cell phone, so I called the number of the store where she worked and asked to speak with her. I heard the person on the phone tell Emily in a quiet but concerned voice, "Your mom wants to talk to you, and she sounds really upset."

There was rustling as Emily took the phone. "Mom?" Emily said, her voice rising with fear. She knew that it must be bad news if I was calling at work.

"Are you somewhere private?" I asked, not wanting to tell her that her sister was dying, while she stood in the middle of the store.

"I'm outside, is Melissa okay?"

"Honey, you need to come to the hospital. The doctor said that Melissa is not doing well. Her heart is getting tired and it's eventually going to just stop beating." I had started to cry, "You can't come to her room, but I know that you will want to be with us afterwards."

"I'm coming," Emily said as she rushed back into the store.

The manager must have seen the look on her face because I heard him say, "Just go."

"I'm getting my purse and I will be there as soon as I can."

"Please drive carefully," I begged, "I can't lose both of you."

Emily promised that she would drive the speed limit and would be very careful, but how careful can you be when you have just been told that your sister is dying?

I had to call Melissa's dad, Eric, who was already dealing with his father, who was ill. He was in Kentucky with his mom and sister but was rushing to the airport and would arrive later this evening.

He texted me back several minutes later to tell me that his mom had reached out to her prayer group and her church, and his sister had reached out to hers. His cousins had reached out to their churches, and one of them had asked the Deacon of her family church for a prayer request but had told him that the request was urgent and couldn't wait until the end of the service. The prayer request started off the service and before long, these requests combined with prayer groups from California, Florida, and all the other states that had been reached, grew to be over one thousand beautiful, loving people, hoping and praying for a miracle for Melissa.

By this time Ian had arrived at the hospital. He rushed into the room, out of breath, and came to stand beside me. The nurse motioned for us to come out of the room shortly after Ian arrived. We stepped out the door and were met by one of

Melissa's doctors, and the nurse that had hurried me into the room when I had first arrived that morning.

The doctor asked, "Do you want to make Melissa a DNR?" The question was asked so abruptly and without any preparation.

The nurse explained further that Melissa's heart was going to give out. It could be now or two hours from now, but it was going to happen. If there was not a Do Not Resuscitate order in place, they would have no choice but to do CPR. They may be able to restart her heart, but it will just be more of the same. She understood that what they were asking us to do was a horrible choice to have to make, but we would need to make it quickly.

I looked at Ian and he looked at me. They were asking us to make the decision to allow my first-born, and the mother of his children, to just die. How does a mother and a fiancée make that kind of decision? Were we supposed to just sit there and hold her hand as the heart in her body stopped beating? How could we sit there and watch that happen and do nothing? I wanted so badly to change places with her. I wanted her to live the life that she had not yet lived. I wanted her to get married, to watch her babies grow up and go to prom. If I could have forfeited my life, so that she could live hers, I would have done so.

As agonizing as it was, Ian and I knew that to try and keep her in this world with us would be selfish, and we needed to make the decision that would be best for Melissa. Although it was the hardest decision that we had ever had to make, the DNR was signed.

I went back to sitting on that hard fold-out chair with Melissa's left hand grasped in mine. Ian was standing next to me with his hand on Melissa's leg. I held her hand up to my cheek and let her know that we were both there. We told her that we knew she was getting tired, and that if she needed to let go it would be okay. Ian was stoic, but I could see the strain on his face. I on the other hand, was a sobbing, snotty mess.

We sat in the room for maybe twenty minutes watching Melissa and all her monitors. We could see her heart rate increase, trying to counteract the fact that despite the ventilator, her blood oxygen level kept steadily going down. We knew that it would not be long. I was angry. I was angry at that little voice of hope, the one that had been whispering in my ear, the one that had told me over and over that everything would be okay. I was angry because that little voice had lied. It had allowed me to feel hope, but that hope had now been pulled out from underneath me, and nothing would ever be okay again.

As I sat there waiting for my oldest child's heart to stop beating, I could see and hear such commotion in the hallway outside Melissa's room. A crowd of scrub-clad men and woman had gathered to include twenty or thirty people. I noticed this group because it felt so unreal that while Melissa was dying the hospital and its staff was still business as usual. I knew in my head that of course life continued on as normal, but it felt to me that everyone and everything else, except Melissa, faded and disappeared, as if it were just the three of us—Ian, Melissa, and me.

The same nurse, the one who had dressed me and had asked about the DNR, once again, opened the door and motioned for us to come out. As we stepped out, several people that had been part of the crowd of people outside Melissa's door, rushed in. One of the doctors disconnected the ventilator, placed a bag over Melissa's intubation tube, and started to squeeze, manually pushing oxygen into her lungs. I was scared and I did not know what was happening.

I walked out of that room with anger growing in my chest until I felt like it would explode. My daughter is lying in this bed dying, and they are asking us to come out of the room again. I didn't know how much longer I had with my daughter, and at this moment my anger hurt less than my anguish, so I allowed it to flow through my body like smoke. The anger filled every cell as it seeped through me. I was angry at everyone, and I was preparing to unload my anger on whoever stood outside that door.

The anger that had been burning inside my chest dissipated as Ian and I stepped out of the room and came face to face with a doctor that we had never seen before. The doctor was an older man in his fifties. He was wearing the typical light blue scrubs and a white lab coat that most of the doctors wore, but I did not remember seeing him before. He pushed his fingers through his gray streaked hair before folding his hands as if he were going to pray, and then he placed his fingertips to his lips. "My name is Doctor Martin, and I am the head of the ECMO department."

Ian looked at me, not understanding why I had just put my face in my hands and started to cry. My sobs were a combination of tremendous relief coupled with gratefulness that the voice had not lied, and disappointment that I had not trusted that little voice. I did not need the doctor to continue, because I already knew that Melissa was going to get her miracle.

"We had to make a very difficult decision just now. Melissa is going to die today if we don't do something. I can't in good conscience allow that to happen without giving her every chance possible."

While Ian and I had been sitting with Melissa, he had gathered all of the nurses from the ventilator floor and nurses and respiratory therapists from the ECMO floor. He let them know that if Melissa was given this machine, they would be working severely shorthanded. He would need to take nurses from the already understaffed ventilator floor and give them to the ECMO unit. They would all have bigger patient loads and they would have to work overtime. The nurses were unanimous in their decision that they all wanted Melissa to have this chance.

"Melissa has essentially won the lottery today because we are giving her the one available machine," he stated.

Melissa was on day nine of the ventilator. I knew that once someone hits day ten, they are no longer eligible for the machine because the longer they are mechanically ventilated the lower their odds of surviving, even with ECMO. I was sad, and I grieved for all the other people who were hoping for that machine and would not survive. I knew the helplessness and desperation that was felt by every loved one of a COVID patient because I had felt it.

I was grateful that the mathematical equation that estimated survival was just a bit higher for Melissa.

Dr. Martin continued on, explaining to us that ECMO was not a sure thing, and that it only increases her odds of survival to about fifty percent. I thought to myself, that's a heck of a lot better than zero percent, which is what the case was without the machine.

The goal of ECMO was to keep Melissa alive long enough to give her lungs time to recover. We would have to hope that they would recover enough to be able to be removed from ECMO and work on their own. If they didn't, she will need to go on the transplant list, but lungs were not an organ that were easy to find at this time.

The ECMO team arrived quickly, and we were left standing outside the door. We couldn't see anything because the curtain had been drawn across the window in the hall. It took about thirty minutes for the nurse to come out and tell us that they had finished, and Melissa would be taken to a different floor shortly. She said that she was going to escort us to the family waiting room on a different floor, and they would let us know when we would be allowed to see her.

As we walked out of the door and into the waiting room for Melissa's current room, I saw my husband waiting for us. He stood up quickly as we walked out. He was not aware that a machine had become available and that it had been given to Melissa. When I told him, he wrapped his arms around me in relief and just held me. I could feel him taking deep breaths, and I felt that at that moment, in his arms, everything was going to be okay.

We all followed the nurse to the new floor and into the waiting room. She said that she would come get us when they got Melissa settled in her room, and they would allow all three of us to see her briefly, but only I would be allowed to stay. I called my youngest daughter, who was still driving, to let her know that Melissa had received the life-saving machine.

I texted both my sisters and my two best friends, "They found Melissa a spot on the ECMO floor. They had me say goodbye to her this morning because she was not going to make it through the end of the day. We had already made the decision to make her a DNR and then they finally told us about the ECMO. They are doing the procedure now. There are a lot of risks, but she will not live without it. I just can't believe that this is happening. It's a nightmare, and I can't wake up!"

Alexandra's Worries

I don't think people are telling me everything. They feel like I can't handle hearing the truth because I'm only 9 years old, so they only tell me the parts they think I can handle. I really want to know the truth, but I don't know the right questions to ask. If they aren't telling me everything, it must be really bad.

Chapter Eight

The ECMO Circuit

September 5, 2021

Once the new nurse settled Melissa in her room and had familiarized herself with Melissa's case, she came to the waiting area to bring us to the room. We walked through double brown doors that opened with a swipe of the nurse's badge. To the left of the hallway were six small glass rooms. On the right was the nurse's station. We stopped in front of room five.

Dr. Z, the doctor in charge of the patients on the ECMO floor, walked over to us to introduce himself. After a brief discussion, I asked, "Is it possible to live with only one lung?"

"Yes, but both her lungs are damaged," he replied, sounding confused by my question.

"I know, but can't I give her one of mine? You said that she could live with only one lung?" He told me that lung donation didn't work that way and I could not give her one of mine. My question was out of desperation, but I would have done anything if it meant keeping her alive.

My heart hurt. There was nothing I could do to help my child live. My chest felt tight, and it was hard to stop crying long enough to finish speaking with the doctor.

My husband and Ian stood for a few minutes looking at Melissa through the window before the nurse walked them out of the unit. I was told that I could go in and sit with Melissa, but only until 10:00 p.m. when visiting hours ended.

I walked into the small, dark room and forced myself to look at my daughter. It was bad enough that she had the IV tubing, breathing tube, feeding tube, and an arterial line, but now a fresh horror added to the mix of medical equipment that was keeping Melissa alive. Next to the foot of her bed was the ECMO machine. It looked like the engine of a car, but instead of oil being circulated, it was Melissa's blood. There was a clear plastic cannula (plastic tube), that was placed in the femoral vein of her right leg. That tube removed deoxygenated blood and sent it through the ECMO machine to regulate the temperature. After filtering her blood, it added oxygen and removed carbon dioxide. The machine then sent the blood back into her body through a second tube that was placed in an artery, accessed through her neck, right above her clavicle.

The ECMO tubing was large. It was the size of a small hose and became narrow as it entered a stainless-steel ring that was stitched into her skin. The cannula looped around by her ear and attached to her neck with a thick suture pushed through her skin and then twisted to keep it secure. There was a big red "IN CASE OF ACCIDENTAL DECANNULATION" sign taped to the machine.

I was afraid to touch her. I was afraid to move. One wrong step to my left and I could unplug her ventilator. One wrong step to my right and I could unplug the ECMO machine, or even worse, step on the tubing, causing it to come out of her body. I made my way to the other side of the bed, being careful to step over the power cords. I lifted the wooden chair off the wall and surveyed the room to determine the safest place for me to set it down. This brown wooden fold out chair, with its ugly green vinyl seat and backrest, had been the one thing throughout the entire ordeal that had remained constant. It was always there, always hard, and always hurt my back.

The room was narrow, and there was only a small walkway on each side of the bed. I decided that to the left of the bed was my best option.

I sat looking at my daughter. She depended on this machine for her life, and I tried to see the good in it. I tried to push away the heavy weight of dread and fear and focus on Melissa. Instead of focusing on the woman who may not live, I tried to remember the little girl. The one who loved to catch fireflies in her Gran and Papa's backyard, only to let them go a few minutes later so that they could go home to their babies.

I remembered the seven-year-old girl who had taken her baby sister out of the crib and put her in a bouncy seat on my bedroom floor. She had made Emily's bottle and settled in to watch cartoons, allowing me to sleep. She had done this quietly, and I slept through all of it.

I remembered the young girl who would always help me with the dishes even when I didn't ask, and I saw the young lady who was so excited to go dress shopping for her Sadie Hawkins dance in junior high. She was so proud of her beautiful blue dress, and it still hangs in my bedroom closet because I can't let it go.

These memories of Melissa are both beautiful and painful. I was fearful that there may be no future memories to make. I sat there for the rest of the afternoon with my face buried in my hands.

Donny had rented a hotel room for the three of us for the night because there was not room for everyone at Melissa's apartment. Emily, Donny, and I sat on the bed eating pizza and watching TV. We only talked a little about Melissa, but she was foremost in all of our minds. It was comforting to have Donny and Emily with me because, while they were with me, I knew they were safe.

Melissa's dad Eric had also rented a room but at a different hotel. He had arrived too late to see Melissa, but I'm sure that, like all the rest of us, it just felt better to be close to the hospital.

September 6, 2021

This morning, I made my way from the parking lot and up to the ECMO floor. I stepped into the elevator and pushed the correct floor number for Melissa's room. Just before the doors closed, a doctor stopped them with his arm and stepped in. He greeted me and made a joke about the weather. I replied, and a brief conversation ensued. It was nice to have a conversation, even a short one with a stranger, that had nothing to do with COVID.

As the doors opened on the 5th floor, he motioned for me to step through the open doors before him and then followed me down the same hallway. I stopped in front of the double doors to Melissa's unit and pushed the call button. The ECMO floor is a locked unit, so the nurse has to let you in. The doctor stopped with me at the door and asked if I had a family member in this unit. He asked this with sympathy, because he already knew that this unit was only for COVID patients.

It was hard not to cry when I answered, but I gave him a short answer about Melissa and why she was here. He put his hand on my shoulder. "I am so sorry," he whispered. "I will keep you both in my thoughts." And then he walked away. I watched as he swiped his badge and walked into the cardiac unit.

Melissa's nurse for the day was in the room, hanging a bag of blood on Melissa's IV pole as I walked in. "Good morning!" she greeted me and then explained that Melissa's hemoglobin was low, so the doctors had ordered the blood to help raise her levels.

I looked at the bed where Melissa lay. It was so hard to see my daughter like this. I hated the thought that if she woke up, she was going to bear the pain and discomfort that was bound to be in her future, but even knowing that I wanted her to wake up. We would deal with the recovery.

I sat down in the wooden chair with nothing but my thoughts. I did not like to be alone with my thoughts because they would go deep into darkness, and I could not control them, so I tried to keep my mind busy.

While sitting there next to Melissa's bed, my mind wandered, settling on Ivy, and how much she had already changed in just three weeks. It occurred to me I could print out all the pictures that Ian and I had taken since the day Ivy was born and make a photo album. When Melissa woke up, she could see all the pictures. It was exciting to think about my new project and hoped that Melissa could see it soon.

Oddly enough, later this afternoon, I received a Facebook message from Jennifer Hanson of Hanson Photography, who was the photographer that had taken my and Donny's wedding photos four years ago. We had remained friends on Facebook, and I so enjoyed seeing all the newborn photos she would post. Newborns were her specialty. She must have read my recent post about Melissa.

She was asking how Melissa was doing and wanted to know if we had gotten newborn photos of Ivy done. If we hadn't, she wanted to do a photo shoot for free. She was a mother and understood how fleeting and precious those first few weeks were, and she wanted to document that time for Melissa. It was a very sweet and thoughtful offer, and we were happy to take her up on it. I could add her pictures to the front of the photo album I would make for Melissa.

September 7, 2021

The ECMO floor is an intensive care unit with nurses that have extensive training. There is one nurse per room, and all five of the ECMO patients on this floor share an ECMO technician, a specialized doctor, nurse practitioner, and several respiratory therapists.

Melissa's nurse has been the same for the three days that she has been on this floor. It was nice to have the same person several days in a row and having a human connection with the nurses was the knot that kept me from unraveling. I had so many people to lean on, people that loved me and loved Melissa, yet I felt alone. I was in the middle of a hospital, a sea of people, but I felt alone. My world had stopped. It was as if a huge, menacing shadow had blanketed the world, and everything had paused. Everyone and everything became still. People stopped existing except for my little circle of family and close friends. I focused my vision only on my daughter lying in that bed. My only goal was for her to live.

I had learned that several of the nurses working on this floor are traveling nurses. They take assignments for several weeks at a time before deciding if they wanted to move on or stay where they were. Melissa's nurse, Star, and I were talking about her experience as a traveling nurse. She told me she could only work for six weeks at a time before having to take several weeks off. Most of the patients that were now on ECMO floors across the country were there because of COVID and most of them did not survive. After caring for the patients, and their family member, it was heartbreaking when they died, and she needed the break.

Wendy Reese

I had been sitting in the room for four or five hours on this day when Star came in to check on Melissa. Before she left the room, she mentioned she did not remember seeing me leave the room, nor did she ever see me eating. Once I admitted I had not left the floor for lunch or dinner, she insisted I do so now. She jokingly took to threats of not letting me back on the floor unless I brought proof that I had eaten.

I knew I needed to feed my body, but just the thought of eating made me feel sick and I worried that something would happen while I was gone. She promised she would watch for me and let me in when I returned, but she wanted me to leave the floor and eat a proper meal. As I approached the cafeteria and smelled the food, my stomach grumbled. I realized I was indeed hungry, so I purchased a meal and took it outside to eat. I had not seen the light of day for so long, except through the hospital window, and it was nice to feel the sun on my shoulders as I ate.

It was funny how just the simple act of eating a certain food could bring on memories. Eric had been at work, and it was just Melissa, Emily, and me. Melissa and I ordered a pizza to be delivered. Melissa asked if she could go out and get the pizza when the delivery person came to the door, so I told her she could. It was very exciting to be allowed such responsibility, and she rushed to the door before the young man with the pizza could even knock. She stepped outside the glass front doors as I watched. She looked so grown up as she handed the man his tip. He bent down to give her the pizza and walked away. By this time, our Lab Richard, who Melissa had named all by herself, smelled the yummy pizza and jumped up on his hind legs trying to get into the box that Melissa was holding. She turned left and right, trying to keep him from getting to the food, but he was very persistent. After just a few seconds of this, she decided she would turn the pizza box sideways and put it under her arm. This was a great idea and would have worked if she had turned the box so that the part that opened was under her arm. Instead, the pizza slipped out of the bottom of the box and landed on the ground right in front of Richard. He ate a good portion of the pizza before I could get out the door to help. Melissa stood watching Richard eat the pizza and cried. I reassured Melissa that it could have happened to anyone, and we would call and order another one. When I explained to the restaurant why we needed a second pizza, they delivered a new one for free.

I returned to Melissa's room thirty minutes later without the jokingly requested proof because I had eaten every bite. The nurse let me in even though I had eaten the proof. Her sense of humor was a pleasant break from the stress.

When visiting hours were over for the evening, I headed back to the apartment. Ian's mom, Angela, otherwise known as Nona, had arrived. She had come up from West Palm Beach to see the baby and to provide support for Ian. As I walked into Harley's room to say goodnight, Nona and Harley were all snuggled up in Harley's bed. They had tucked the purple comforter around them. Nona was reading a goodnight story and Harley was listening intently. I left the room so as not to disturb them.

September 8, 2021

I once again took my position in the wooden folding chair next to the bed. The room and nurses differed from the ventilator floor, but the fear was the same. Ian and I lived every day with the fear that the ECMO machine may not work, and we would have put Melissa through this for nothing.

I did not know how the ECMO and ventilator worked together, so I asked everyone who stepped into that room for every bit of information that I could get. I would ask the same questions over and over, and they would always answer like it was the first time that I had asked. Some were better at explaining things, but they all tried.

Dr. Z came in throughout the day to check on Melissa. I'm not sure if he ever went home. If he was not in the room checking in on Melissa, I could always see him in the hallway speaking with a nurse, or in another patient's room. While he was checking on Melissa, I used the time to question him about how she was doing and his expectations for her progress.

The hope for Melissa was that they would see improvement over the next fourteen days. If her blood gases did not improve and the ECMO machines settings lowered by that time, we would know that the gas exchange was not happening appropriately in her lungs. We would then have different decisions to make. I tried not to think about that, but the thought was always lurking right around the corner. The thought was my constant shadow, and I could not get away from it.

Along with improvements in her blood gas, they were also looking at the volume of Melissa's inspiration. Because her lungs were stiff from scar tissue, the doctors wanted to be very careful with the volume of oxygen pushed into her lungs. If they pushed too much, her lungs could not stretch to accommodate the volume. Not enough oxygen would cause brain damage. Right now, they could only push seventy milliliters of oxygen, but it needed to be upwards of three hundred milliliters. She still had a very long way to go.

Once I learned this bit of information, I would sit in the chair and watch the ventilator monitor to see the volume of every breath. I would try to breathe with her, filling my lungs as if I could help her take a deeper breath. I felt that if I willed it enough, the number would climb. Sometimes it did.

The nurses lowered Melissa's sedation earlier today. She had not responded well. The doctor wanted to allow her to wake and be able to take part in her care but waking up with an intubation tube was difficult. They needed her awake enough, even if just for a moment, to do a neurological assessment. The doctors wanted to see if she would open her eyes or wiggle fingers or toes, but the nurse said that Melissa just wasn't ready. They would try again later.

Melissa would need to be on the ventilator for weeks, if not several months. Her doctors had requested a consult to evaluate Melissa for a tracheotomy. Although a breathing tube inserted through a tracheostomy in her neck would be uncomfortable, it would be better than having a breathing tube down her throat. The determination was that her oxygen level was not high enough to tolerate being without oxygen for the several seconds it would take to insert the tube. They would have to wait several days and re-evaluate her.

I had to leave a little early today, so I gathered my things and waited for the doctor to round. I left as soon as he finished his evaluation of Melissa. Melissa's dad was at the apartment when I arrived. Harley was a bundle of energy, so we took her outside in a little used part of the parking lot and let her play with a bottle of bubbles. She would dip the wand into the soapy liquid and then spin around in a circle with her arm stretched out, making the bubbles swirl around her body. As she spun, she made a high-pitched woooo.

Harley handed Eric the wand and commanded, "You do it!" What else does any grampa worth his salt do when a three-year-old hands him bubbles? He took the wand from her outstretched hand, spun around on one foot, and made the same woooo sound Harley had made. She loved it!

September 9, 2021

The ringing of my phone jarred me from sleep early this morning. As I frantically reached for the phone, I hoped it would be a wrong number and not the hospital with bad news. Holding my breath, I answered the call. It was Dr. Z. He was calling to ask if I had the phone number for Melissa's OB because Melissa was having some vaginal bleeding. He wanted the OB to check on her just to make sure that it was normal postpartum bleeding, and not something more ominous. As long as Melissa was on ECMO, she had to be on blood thinners to help prevent blood clots from sticking to the sides of the ECMO tubing, and he wanted to make sure that there was no internal bleeding.

Blood clots and infection were the two enormous dangers of the ECMO circuit, and the blood thinners were necessary; however, there was a fine line between preventing the clots from forming and thinning Melissa's blood so much that she was at risk of internal bleeding.

When Dr. Z. called to speak with the OB, she was concerned about Melissa and said that she would come by later in the evening to check on her.

I waited all day for the OB to arrive, but eventually stepped out to run to the cafeteria. When I got back to the room, the nurse said that the OB had already been. She had determined that it was just normal post-baby discharge, and she saw nothing to worry about. I still worried though because I felt that every time Melissa was on a smooth path, something would always happen and cause a bump. There was never a time that I could relax, and I was always on the lookout for the next bit of bad news.

Chapter Nine

The Faces Behind the Mask

September 11, 2021

I arrived this morning to find that they had removed the isolation protocol sign from the door to Melissa's room! This meant that they no longer had to treat her as if she were contagious.

A pink surgical mask replaced the brown respirators that had hidden the nurses' faces from view, and I could get a better idea of what each nurse looked like. It's funny how my brain had filled in the missing part of each person's face (the part covered by the mask) but had been totally inaccurate. They looked nothing like what my brain had imagined. Those beautiful, tired faces belonged to the heroes who had cared so lovingly for my daughter.

They left the sliding glass door to the room open so that I could see and hear the bustling of the busy unit. Best of all, I was no longer required to wear the hot isolation gown, the goggles that fogged up when I cried, and the N95 mask that had rubbed the bridge of my nose and chin raw. I did not have to remove the gear every time that I needed to use the restroom or go downstairs to make phone calls, only to put it back on when I returned.

    My favorite ECMO technician was working today, and that meant that I could add to the limited knowledge that I had gained so far. He was the best at explaining how things worked and what to expect. Although I had some medical experience, the tubes, machines, and settings were all foreign to me, and it was scary. Having someone who would explain how it all worked, over and over, and being able to put things into a context that I could understand, was priceless. If I could not visualize something that he was explaining, he would draw a diagram on the window that separated Melissa's room from the next. Having a very basic understanding of how the ECMO circuit worked was invaluable for me, as it took some of the scary away.

    Later this evening, the nurses tried once more to wean Melissa from some of the sedation medication, hoping that they could get her to wake up enough to respond to their request to squeeze their fingers or to wiggle her toes, but she did neither. Melissa looked at me with sedation glazed eyes, open wide in panic. She looked at me as if begging for help that I could not give her. Those eyes darted around the room, searching for anything that would be familiar to her. She had been in a medicated coma for the last several weeks and was totally unaware of the events of the last twenty-one days. I hated to see her distress. It was so hard to watch her respiratory rate skyrocketing, or her ventilator tube popping off when she coughed. Her blood pressure would spike as fear permeated her brain. She won't remember this moment, or even the moments and hours and weeks preceding this moment, but I will. My mind screamed in silent desperation, get out! Leave! Run away! Her fear was too much to watch. This was too hard! I wanted to run and hide, but my love for her was stronger than my need to get away from the horror. I gently cupped her face in my hands and whispered in her ear. "Sweet girl you are a fighter, and you are strong. Everything is okay. You are okay." I didn't know if she would be okay, but I really needed her to believe that she would.

She would look into my eyes as I stood over her, but I don't know if she really saw me. Eventually, her eyes would roll back into her head, and she would fall back to sleep, only to wake up again several minutes later. She would repeat this cycle, again and again, until later in the evening when the nurse kept her sedated and let her sleep.

In between comforting Melissa, I was also comforting my youngest, Emily. Papa, one of the people that Emily and Melissa loved most in this world, had just entered hospice. Papa was my ex-husband's father. The doctors had recently diagnosed him with cancer, and he also had a cardiac issue. Papa is a wonderful, loving husband, father, and Papa who, in my 22 years of knowing him, had never uttered an unkind word. He was the kind of father and grandfather that everyone hoped for, but only a few lucky ones got. It devastated Emily.

Emily had flown to Kentucky earlier in August to visit him while he was in the hospital, but Melissa could not go because of her advanced pregnancy. Emily had been so happy when Papa recognized her when she arrived at the hospital. The surgeons were intending to replace a valve in his heart, knowing that if they were successful, it would not only prolong his life but would give him a better quality of life for the time he had left. There was nothing they could do about the cancer. The surgeons could not replace the valve, so Papa went home.

Once again, guilt plagued me. Both my daughters were suffering, just in different ways. I had to choose which one got most of my attention. I spent time on the phone with Emily, discussing her worries and fears, but something always interrupted our conversation when doctors or nurses came in to ask questions or to tell me something about Melissa. Talking to me on the phone was not the same as having mom there to hug you. I knew Emily understood why I couldn't be there with her, but that did not stop me from feeling as if I had failed her.

September 12, 2021

I spent the early afternoon FaceTiming with Alexandra, who was telling me about her day at school.

She was telling me about the play they were working on and showing me a new song that she had just taught herself on the piano. We touched on a lot of subjects while we talked on the phone, but the one thing she had not asked about since the time in the parking garage was how Mommy was. She avoided the subject. If I brought it up, she would change the subject. I assumed it was too hard for her to process what was happening, and avoidance was her way of coping.

I was sitting next to the hospital bed, with the phone in one hand, and holding Melissa's hand in the other. As I sat there listening to Alex talk, I felt Melissa's fingers squeeze. There was just the smallest little flutter in her first and middle fingers. I had been holding her hand all day, for weeks, and never once did her fingers move! After I told Alex that I would call her back I stood up quickly and dropped the phone on the table.

Leaning my face closer to Melissa's ear I asked, "Sweet girl, can you please squeeze my hand?" and joy of all joys, she did. The squeeze was very light, but it was there, and it was deliberate. Maybe hearing Alexandra's voice had spurred something in Melissa's brain, causing her to wake enough to respond.

Dr. Z had scheduled a brain scan later in the day because he was concerned about potential brain damage that the lack of oxygen could have caused, or maybe from being on ECMO. He felt that Melissa should have been able to follow simple commands by now, and he was a little concerned that, as of yet, she had done nothing other than open her eyes.

I went out into the hallway and hunted down Dr. Z to tell him she was responding. He was very excited and came into the room right away, placed two of his fingers in Melissa's hand, and spoke in a very loud voice, "Melissa, squeeze my fingers." There was nothing. Not even a quiver of movement. He asked again, even louder, "Melissa, I need you to squeeze my fingers!" Again, nothing happened. He gave up trying and told me she had just had a muscle twitch and that I had attributed the movement as a response because I wanted it so badly to have been deliberate. Those were not his exact words, but that was basically what he was saying.

I knew it was not wishful thinking. She had done it with deliberation and was right on cue when I asked her to do it. I laughed to myself and thought that maybe if he had used a softer voice, she might have obliged him.

The technicians came in later that afternoon to run the brain scan. They used what looked and felt like petroleum jelly to attach ten or twelve electrodes to her head. The scan ran for about twenty minutes before they pulled the electrodes off her scalp, leaving her already dirty hair with globs of greasy gunk that made the strands stick together as it dried. As they left the room, I resumed my position by the bed.

There was no way that I had imagined her squeeze simply because I wanted it to be true. I had to prove to myself that it had really happened. I placed my fingers in her limp hand and gently called her name and asked her to squeeze my hand. Her eyes opened wide when I called her name, and even though it still looked like she was staring into nothingness, she turned her face toward me and squeezed my hand!

"I saw that!" I heard from the glass sliding door to the room. The nurse practitioner had been coming into the room but stopped at the door, not wanting to interrupt. She had seen the squeeze.

"Do it again!" I asked in excitement, and she did... Hard.

Alexandra's Worries

Grammy let me talk to mommy today. Part of me was afraid that when Grammy turned the phone, I would see mommy with the tube that helps her breathe and that would be scary. The other part of me kind of hoped that I would see her because I love her even if she had a tube. I wasn't really sure what to say to Mommy. Should I just tell her I love her, or should I tell her about my day? My Mama, daddy's mom, helped me figure out what to say. I wanted Mommy to hear me so that she knew how much I loved her.

September 14, 2021

Today, Melissa's intubation tube was going to be replaced and a tracheostomy (trach) in her neck would replace it. The trach team had come back in yesterday to re-evaluate Melissa's oxygen levels. They were higher and staying steady, so they approved the procedure. I was relieved because the ventilator would be much easier to tolerate if she didn't have a tube shoved down her throat through her mouth. The nurses warned me she wouldn't like it when she woke up, but it was the better of two evils.

The surgical team moved Melissa to the operating room instead of doing the procedure bedside. They asked me to step out of the unit and wait in the family waiting area until they brought Melissa back to her room. I had to fight back panic; they were going to cut a hole in her neck and into her windpipe, and it was scary! Everything was scary.

When Hope is Enough

As I sat in the waiting room, I recalled the conversation that I had the night before with Ian. I had arrived home after 10:00 p.m. and was sitting in the rocker holding Ivy. We had already put Harley to bed, and Ian was in the kitchen cleaning up the dinner dishes. I noticed he had been very pensive, but suddenly, he looked up and asked if we were doing the right thing for Melissa? Were we just torturing her because we don't want to let her go?

I had been thinking the same thing earlier this week as I had watched the panic cross Melissa's face every time she woke. I really wasn't sure how to answer him, so I asked him if it was him in the bed and in the same situation, would he want everything possible done for him? If he had a fifty percent chance of surviving and being able to live a normal life, would he want the same decisions to be made for him?

He thought for a minute and confirmed that yes, he would want every measure to be taken if it was possible for him to live normally, without mechanical support, and care for his family.

There was our answer. We were, of course, wanting Melissa to live, but we were not being selfish. We were not keeping her alive knowing that she had no chance of recovery or would depend on machines forever. She had more than a fifty percent chance of surviving and leading a normal life.

The phone rang at the volunteer desk in the family waiting room, pulling me back to reality. There was no one sitting there to answer it, so I did. It was the nurse letting me know Melissa was out of surgery and was being moved back to her room. They would come get me as soon as they settled her in the room.

I left the waiting room and went to lean on the wall in front of the unit doors. As I stood there, two doctors passed by, deep in discussion. I realized as they passed that one of them was the doctor from the elevator yesterday. As they stopped in front of the cardiac unit, the two doctors finished their conversation. The doctor that I did not recognize swiped his ID badge and walked through the doors. The doctor that I had spoken with in the elevator (one of Melissa's nurses had told me the other day that he was the head of the cardiac unit), backed up to stop in front of me and asked how Melissa was doing.

I couldn't believe that he recognized me and even more surprised that he had remembered Melissa's name. It was amazing how this small act of kindness made such a giant impact on me. I told him she was doing as well as can be expected, and that they were just bringing her back from surgery to put her trach in.

He told me he had been thinking about her and said that it was a terrible situation, especially for someone so young. I agreed and thanked him for asking about her. By this time, the nurse had opened the door and motioned for me to come in.

As I walked into Melissa's room my heart melted. There was my daughter's beautiful face, without all the tubing holding her mouth open.

In her neck, right above her collarbone, in the hollow space below the Adam's Apple, was the trach. It was a white oval disk with a tube in the back that went down into her throat about three inches. I was told that there was a small balloon on the bottom of the tube inside of her throat that was expanded with saline solution to help hold it in place. The disk was sutured to her skin on both sides. A strap was clipped to one side of the disk and wrapped around the back of her neck, securing it to the other side, ensuring that it did not come out.

They had pushed gauze under the plastic disk to protect her skin from the plastic and to soak up the blood from the incision. I was very surprised how bloody it was, as I watched it dribble down her neck, into her hair, and onto the pillowcase. The ventilator tube was now attached to the trach. I knew that when she woke up, she would not like it, but for me, it was one step closer to being able to bring my baby home.

September 15, 2021

I arrived a little later than normal today. Ian had to take Ivy to the pediatrician, so I stayed home with Harley until he got back. I sat in the rocker, watching Harley play with her Dat Bam (Batman), making him ride her plastic dinosaurs, and felt a rush of sadness.

I missed my husband and youngest daughter. I missed calling Melissa on the phone and hearing her answer, "Hi Momma!" My heart ached for her to wake up and say those two words. I picked up my cell phone and scrolled through all of my voicemails, thinking that there should be an old message from her. As I searched for her name, I remembered I had recently cleaned all the old voicemails and had deleted them. I called Melissa's phone to hear her voice on her voicemail, but it was a standard, prerecorded message, and not Melissa's voice. I cried in disappointment. It was devastating to think that I might never hear my daughter's voice again.

Harley saw the tears on my cheeks and ran to the bathroom. When she came back out of the bathroom, holding a single square of toilet paper, she placed her hands on my knees and looked up into my face. "It's okay Grammy, it's okay." She patted my knee. "No more crynen. Take a deep breaf." She took a deep breath, demonstrating how I should do it. There was no way that I could not feel a little better after that. What a wonderful, caring child that my daughter and Ian had raised.

When Ian came home with Ivy, he smiled at us and said the report from the pediatrician was that Ivy was perfect. The smile did not quite reach his eyes though, and I knew he wished Melissa could have gone to the appointment with him.

Chapter Ten

As One Life is Ending

September 16, 2021

I talked with the night nurse around 5:00 a.m. just to check on Melissa. She told me they had cut back on the amount of sedation that Melissa was receiving, and she was not tolerating it well. The nurse said Melissa may be opening her eyes and getting agitated, but she was still pretty sedated. She would not remember this moment in time, and I should not hurry to the hospital. Hurry was exactly what I was going to do. I don't know for sure how much of Melissa was there in her sedated brain, but surely there would be some part of her brain that would recognize my voice.

When I arrived, her heart and respiratory rate, as well as her blood pressure were elevated. As soon as I walked into the room, picked up her hand, and reassured her that she was okay, she calmed down.

Shortly after I arrived, my husband texted, asking how Melissa and I were doing this morning. I really wanted to tell him we were great, but that would not have been the truth. It had been a very stressful morning, and I was feeling very emotional. I told him they had taken away so much of Melissa's sedation that she was very restless. My worry was that she was having pain, but there really was no way of confirming that. I was also anxious that Emily would call with the news that Papa had passed. I wanted to be there with her when she learned of Papa's passing, but that was impossible. My sweet husband assured me he would be there for Emily should she need him.

Dr. Z came in to check on Melissa a little later. The nurses had successfully solicited a response from Melissa. She had wiggled her toes and squeezed fingers for the nurses, but she had not done it for Dr. Z, so he was doubtful. He stepped to the side of the bed and said, "Melissa, squeeze my fingers!" still using the same loud voice as last time....nothing. "Melissa, I think you don't like me because you will squeeze everyone else's fingers, but not mine. Please squeeze my fingers." We could all see as Melissa's fingers closed around the doctors' and squeezed tight.

Such a small little thing to squeeze someone's fingers, but for Melissa, it was like she had just planted a flag on the moon. She was showing the doctors and nurses who had made the difficult decision to give the one available machine to Melissa that they had made the right choice. Her will to live was stronger than COVID, and right now we all felt elated! I couldn't wait to tell Ian!

As the day went on, and more of the sedation wore off, Melissa made a drastic improvement. She was awake for longer periods of time and even though I would have to stand over her and tell her that everything was okay; she was getting better. The improvements on the lung x-ray that was taken that morning were astounding. Where once there had been only cloudy white scar tissue, now had small, black open areas. Her lungs were clearing, and along with that, her blood gasses were improving.

It was that afternoon that Emily called to tell me Papa was gone. As Melissa was rejoining the world, Papa had left it. Earlier this morning, the doctor said that Melissa had just turned an important corner in her recovery. I couldn't help but wonder if Papa had a hand in her improvement, helping her, as their spirits passed each other. I don't know how death works, but it was astounding to me that as soon as Papa left the world as we know it, Melissa started improving by leaps and bounds. Papa was an extraordinary man, and it would not be surprising that he would delay his reward to help Melissa.

Again, I felt I had failed my youngest by not being with her while she was suffering the loss of someone that she loved so dearly. Although she is technically an adult, to me she is still a young girl who needed her mother, and I wasn't there. Emily is stronger than she knows and can handle more than she thinks she can, and I am so proud of her in how she handled this loss.

Papa's wife, son, daughter, and close family had surrounded him as he passed. Gran, having just suffered a great loss, was still messaging me for updates on Melissa. She had sent several messages that had provided comfort to me, and her strength amazed me.

I dreaded that at some point I was going to have to tell Melissa that her Papa had passed, but not today.

September 17, 2021

When I walked into Melissa's room this morning, it was different from any other morning so far. Instead of looking at my still, lifeless daughter, I was looking into her beautiful eyes, and she was looking back at me. She couldn't speak with the trach in place, and she was weak from her extended illness and the ECMO, but she was seeing me!

We had all been told from the beginning of ECMO that if Melissa survived, she would be profoundly weak. The doctors had said that most of the patients who survived ECMO would not be strong enough to perform day-to-day tasks for up to a year. Melissa would have to learn to walk and perform other tasks and would require extensive in-patient physical therapy to get as close to full mobility as possible.

I really didn't want Melissa to have to stay at a rehab facility. The doctors tried really hard to convince me that it would be better for her to stay in the facility rather than going home with me. I was not convinced, but for the moment, I let it go.

I had noticed several beds in the hallway when I arrived this morning but did not know why they were there. Dr. Z came in and excitedly told me about his new acquisitions. The beds that lined the hallway were stand up therapy beds. With these beds, they could place a patient in a weight bearing position before they were completely awake. There were five new beds and a representative from the bed company to help instruct the nurses on how to use them.

When it was Melissa's turn, they transferred her from her old bed into the new one. This was not accomplished easily, and it left her feeling tired and grumpy. Dr. Z insisted we proceed with the standup therapy. Two wide blue neoprene strips were crisscrossed over Melissa's knees and then secured to cut outs in the bed's side. Two on each side, one close to her hips and one down by her ankles.

The technician explained to Melissa that he was going to raise the head of the bed, and she may feel like she was sliding out the bottom. Her feet would land on a platform at the foot of the bed, allowing weight to be transferred to her legs and feet. He spoke to her as a courtesy, but she was not aware enough to understand what was being explained. As her body slid down, she jerked awake, as the feeling of falling was new to her. She was not at all happy with the technician, or the bed, and this caused her heart and respiratory rate to increase.

Star, her nurse for the day, was standing with me. Melissa's distress was difficult for both of us to watch. "This is ridiculous!" Star exclaimed, as she pushed the button on the IV pole, giving Melissa a dose of sedation. Star did not feel that it was necessary for Melissa to have to endure an hour of suffering, and I agreed with her wholeheartedly.

The medication was strong enough that Melissa soon fell asleep. I was so grateful to Star for her compassion. We could explain why things were being done, but Melissa didn't really understand, so she was reasonably upset. It was not fun for any of us to watch. The bed was eventually lowered, the straps removed, and they left Melissa to rest for the afternoon.

By the time Melissa woke, she had gained a little more movement in her neck and arms. She would turn her head, and I could tell that she was looking for me. I would stand up, reassure her, and then sit back down. Sometimes she would lift her forearms off of the bed, trying to reach up for the ventilator tubing, but she couldn't quite get close enough to reach it. She was still very sedated and wasn't really aware that she had a trach or was on a ventilator. She just knew that something was in her throat, and it was uncomfortable.

Within a few hours, she was getting her hands pretty close to the feeding tube in her nose and the ventilator tubing that draped across her chest. Although she could lift her arms at the elbow, she had no use of her hands. She couldn't deliberately move her fingers to grasp anything. Until she could use her fingers, I would have to hope that she wouldn't be able to pull anything out just by lifting her arms and getting her fingers accidently stuck in one of the tubes.

Melissa had been chemically restrained with strong sedation medication. There were wires and tubes everywhere attaching her to machines or pumps and keeping her from turning or moving. The last thing I wanted to do was to restrain her by holding her hands down. I chose to extend my arm across her chest so that when she was able to lift her arms high enough, my arm would prevent hers from reaching anything that could cause harm. I could only hope that it would not cause her to feel restrained any more than she already was.

September 18, 2021

Melissa had been on very strong sedation and narcotic pain medication for weeks, and I was very concerned about addiction. I knew that the medication was absolutely necessary but that did not stop the worry. Every one of Melissa's nurses said that we would know when it was time to completely turn her sedation. I didn't realize that the cue to turn it off would come directly from Melissa. The nurses had been turning the medication down a little every day, allowing her to wake slowly and to help prevent withdrawals. Today, as Melissa's nurse and I were standing at the head of the bed, Melissa started to shake her head from side to side. It was almost as if she was trying to shake her brain awake. As she shook her head, she whispered, "I need to wake up, but I can't." There really was no sound from her mouth because she still had the trach, but we could clearly see that her lips had said exactly that. She was telling us that it was time for her to wake up completely.

Her nurse immediately reached up and turned off all of the sedation medication. If Melissa was asking to wake up, she needed to be allowed to. She would still need IV pain medication, but it was time for her to wake up.

Wendy Reese

September 19, 2021

Melissa was a little more aware today as the sedation medication worked its way out of her body. The speech therapist had come by to bring some items that might help Melissa to communicate more easily. She was starting to mouth words, but she would really enunciate them, thinking that it would help me understand, but it just distorted the words. I'm sure it was very frustrating that I could not always understand her. Sometimes it took me a long time to guess what she was trying to say. Eventually she would shake her head and wave her arms in front of her chest, as if saying, just forget it.

We started using a laminated piece of 8.5 inch by 11inch paper that had the alphabet written in columns across the paper. I was supposed to point to a row, and she would nod if the letter that she wanted was in that row. As you can imagine, that took a really long time to get just a single word out. Melissa's mind was still very fuzzy, so she couldn't always remember the instructions for how to use the spelling sheet, and sometimes she forgot what word she was spelling. She was still very calm about it and didn't get angry that I couldn't always get what she was saying.

Later that afternoon, the therapist brought in a pointer that was placed inside a leather band. The band wrapped around Melissa's hand and had a pocket that sat on the back of her hand. This allowed the pen to stick out away from her and be used as a pointer. She still had use of only her arms and could not use her hands or fingers to point. With this band, she was able to move her arm enough to point the pen at the paper, although not always very accurately. It still took a while, and a lot of guessing, but we were able to communicate a little better with this method.

Since Melissa was sort of awake, I asked if she wanted to see the picture book that I had made of Ivy. She indicated that she wanted to see it. I pulled the book off of the shelf and held it in front of her, flipping the pages so that she could see her daughter. I really thought that this would bring her joy, but instead of making her smile, it made her cry. She turned her head away and moved her arm in a sideways, back and forth movement, asking me to stop. Her face turned red, and a tear fell from one eye. I felt awful for having pushed things. I should have known that it was too early for her to cope with not being in those pictures holding her newborn daughter. Everyone else was holding Ivy, but Melissa was stuck, helpless, in this bed.

I left the book on the shelf in the room where it was out of her sight, hoping that eventually Melissa would be able to enjoy them. In the meantime, the nurses, respiratory therapists, and the housekeeping staff spent a lot of time flipping through the pages. I had included the photos that the photographer had taken. Everyone commented on how adorable they were.

As the evening wore on, and staff changed for the night shift, I wondered who Melissa's nurse for the evening would be. It was always hard to leave her at night when it was a new person. When the day and night shift nurses came by the room for report, we were introduced to Steve. He was very good natured, very exuberant, and I loved him!

Melissa might not remember much of Steve because even though the sedation had been turned off the day before, she still had a lot of it in her system. It would take several days for her body to be rid of it. I will remember him because he was one of those very special nurses. The kind that you just trust the minute that you meet them. His job was to take care of Melissa, but he also took care of me.

After bringing me the cup of cranberry juice that he had offered me, he laid out his plan for the evening. He wanted to make sure that Melissa was clean, comfortable, and that she received all of her nighttime medications. He also indicated to me that he would be sitting in the room with Melissa instead of sitting at a desk in the nurse's station and just checking in on her. I was relieved that he was planning on staying with her, because I was still afraid that she might pull her ventilator tube off, or the feeding tube out of her nose.

    Melissa was no longer heavily sedated, so we now had a new problem. She was a young woman who now had the wherewithal to realize that there were some very personal matters that would need to be attended to. She was embarrassed and humiliated that, not only did someone have to clean her, but it had to be a male. Steve recognized Melissa's discomfort and addressed it immediately.

    "Melissa, if I was sick and, in this hospital, my coworkers would be cleaning me up. This is my job, and I do it every day. We are in this together, and we will get through it together because we are night shift buddies. Shit happens." He shrugged his shoulders. "You know that, right?" I really loved that he didn't stand over Melissa when speaking to her. Instead, he leaned over the bed, put his elbows on the mattress and used his hands to brace his chin. He didn't loom over her, making her feel powerless. He got down to her level and spoke to her as if they were conspirators.

    Once Steve had Melissa cleaned up and settled in, it was about time for me to leave for the night. I had always had a difficult time leaving because I was afraid something would happen, but never because Melissa didn't want me to leave. Up until this point, she really didn't know if I was there or not, nor did she have any sense of time. As my leaving was mentioned, Melissa's head snapped around to look at me. She then looked at Steve, placed her forearms together, as best as she could, and looked at him pleadingly. She was begging him to let me stay. It was all I could do not to cry and beg him as well. Melissa was now aware enough to be scared and did not want the one person that she was familiar with, to leave. I didn't want to leave either, but I had no choice.

Steve assured Melissa that he would stay in the room with her, and she need not be afraid. If she was really missing me, he would help her FaceTime me even if it were the middle of the night. Sure enough, I heard my phone ring sometime around 3:00 a.m. Melissa couldn't talk to me, so I spoke to her, and she just watched the screen. It was sad that she felt so helpless, but I was glad that Steve was with her and had lived up to his promise.

September 20, 2021

I got to the hospital early this morning because I had worried about Melissa all night. I was assured that she would have very little memory of what happened from day to day. Even so, I couldn't get past the idea that, at this very moment in time, she knew that I was not there, and she was scared.

I didn't want her to feel abandoned, and I really couldn't understand why I was not allowed to stay through the night. I know it has to do with COVID, but I can't figure out what the reasoning is. I am no more a COVID risk to the patients, doctors, or nurses at night than I am during the day. I think that it just made things easier for the staff when all the visitors left for the night.

During the light of day, being left alone was not as hard for Melissa although she didn't like it when I was gone for long. Doctors, nurses, techs, therapists, and housekeeping were in and out all day. The hospital was alive with talking and laughter, doors shutting, and carts rolling by the door. Night was a different story. I am sure that the darkness held a sinister feeling for Melissa, just as it would have for me in the same situation. I could only imagine how she must feel when I go home. The darkness is scary, especially when you are helpless. Not only is she incapable of doing even the smallest thing for herself, she is unable to reach the call light. Even if she was able to reach it, she would not be able to press the button to alert the staff that she needed help.

As I walked down the hallway to Melissa's room, I noticed that several of the rooms that I passed had colorful decorations on the windows that separated each room. I tried really hard not to look into other patients' rooms, but it was difficult not to notice balloons and streamers.

Melissa's room was very drab gray, with nothing of interest to look at. Her bed faced away from the window, so she couldn't even watch the helicopter land on the pad across the street. The television in her room had not worked from the first day of her transfer, and even if it did work, she would not have been able to work the remote. I did, however, think that she may enjoy looking at a colorful window.

I set to work contacting our family and friends, asking them for notes of encouragement, as well as any pictures that they felt were special. I asked for pictures of Melissa with her friends and families. I wanted to hang them on the window so that the nurses could see Melissa as I knew her to be, a beautiful, generous, and happy woman, full of life and light. Everyone who had entered her room had been kind, caring, and completely dedicated to giving Melissa the best chance of recovery. I wanted them to see who she had been before becoming ill.

Before I had finished texting and emailing my request to all of our friends and families, I was already receiving replies. Her very close girlfriends sent notes and photo's that contained special meaning for them. I was even receiving encouraging notes to Melissa from friends of friends. People that I had never met were sending this wonderful outpouring of love and encouragement, and I was so incredibly grateful and deeply touched.

The window was decorated with pink construction paper and all of the pictures and cards that had been sent. Some of the pictures were from her high school years. Some were from a wedding that she had attended just months ago, and some were of Melissa with her two older daughters and her fiancé. All of the pictures showed a vibrant young woman, and the staff enjoyed looking at them. Everyone who walked into her room always ended up standing in front of the little window, reading the notes and looking at the pictures. It gave them a little window into Melissa's life before COVID.

Wendy Reese

Chapter Eleven

Who Said I Wanted to Die

September 21, 2021

I woke up early this morning feeling so exhausted. Spending hour upon hour, day after day, sitting in the wooden fold-out chair was taking a toll. The past four weeks of constant, agonizing worry was preventing me from sleeping and eating properly, and exhaustion was catching up.

    I stood looking at myself in the mirror and didn't recognize the woman looking back. I looked old and tired. There was no spark of life. As I stood there, I wondered if I would ever see my daughter's grin or hear her laugh again. I would have given anything to hear her voice, instead of whispered words, even if it were to chastise me for saying something that she disagreed with. I hated COVID…with every fiber of my being…and I just wanted it to go away and leave my daughter alone!

    As I walked down the hallway to Melissa's room, I was met by her nurse for the day. She was rushing toward me, and I was afraid that some unknown disaster was about to be announced. It shocked me when she told me that Melissa had been disconnecting her ventilator tube and telling them she wanted to die.

I was so taken aback by what she had just told me, and I couldn't believe that what she was saying was true. If it were true, why did they not call me or Ian to let us know? Melissa had a long road to recovery. She had some very daunting things to get through, but her prognosis was looking more and more positive. I could not believe that what the nurse was telling me was true.

Melissa's eyes were open when I stepped into the room, and she looked very upset. I asked her if she could tell me what was wrong and what had happened during the night. We pieced things together using the spelling sheet, pantomime, and some lip reading. When I asked Melissa about wanting to die, she looked at me like I had grown two heads. In confusion, she lifted her hands, palms up, and raised her shoulders. There was consternation on her face as Melissa shook her head and mouthed that she had not said that. She had pulled the ventilator tubing off because the machine would register that it was disconnected and sound an alarm. When the alarm went off, a nurse would come quickly. The nurse would reconnect the breathing tube and ask Melissa if she wanted to die. Melissa was trying to tell her that no, she did not want to die, but the nurse misunderstood.

I am not sure if Melissa had needed help or if she was just scared and needed someone just to be with her. She could not push the call light, she could not wave her arms or get out of bed, and she could not ask for help. What she could do was push her arm through the ventilator tube and dislodge it, prompting an alarm.

Fortunately, by this time, I was pretty sure that Melissa could maintain her own airway, at least for short periods of time. Not being on the ventilator for those short times had caused no problem for her. I'm sure it caused a big problem for her nurse. The hospital and the ECMO floor were completely full, overwhelming the nurses with patients. Somehow, they still gave exceptional care. I was so grateful for all of them.

Once we straightened out the misunderstanding, the day got a little better. The doctors were planning on removing the stitches that held Melissa's trach in place, and we hoped that removing the stitches might make it more comfortable. The trach strap would still have to be attached to hold the trach inside the hole in her throat, but the strap was soft and didn't have to be tight.

It was a little disconcerting to have the stitches removed because Melissa started to cough. The cough was very aggressive and would last for several seconds, leaving her breathless as her oxygen level lowered. Fortunately, the level would come right back up when the coughing stopped. Sometimes the cough was so strong that the force of it created enough pressure to pop the ventilator tubing off of the trach. I would sit by the bed and watch the tubing pop off, grab it, and put it back on. She would have only a few minutes to recover before another coughing fit started.

It wasn't until the ECMO technician came in during the afternoon and pointed out that they had turned the ECMO machine down that I realized how well Melissa was doing. Despite the horrible cough, she was still maintaining her oxygen levels. In the first few days of ECMO the machine ran at a level ten, doing all the work for her. It was slowly lowered, until finally it would be turned off. Today, they had it set at two. Her lungs were doing most of the work, and her oxygen levels were staying steady, except during the coughing fits. Once they could get the setting to zero, they would monitor her for twenty-four hours. Once they were sure she could maintain her oxygen and carbon dioxide levels, they would remove the ECMO tubing from her neck and groin.

They stopped saying, *if* we can get her weaned off, and replaced it with *when*. They were now sure that her lungs had recovered enough that they could eventually work on their own. Melissa had a long road to travel, but at least I knew she would get to travel that road. It wasn't until this moment that I knew my daughter was going to live.

September 22, 2021

Now that we were feeling confident that Melissa would eventually go home, I shifted my focus to a new concern. I expressed my concern to the nurse about how Melissa might feel when she realized it had been almost five weeks since Ivy's birth. I was worried about how she would handle having missed this time with her. Newborns change so much in five weeks, and you can't erase the passage of time.

Ian and Melissa had made plans for Ivy's outfit and pictures because they were so excited to bring her home. Melissa had really wanted to nurse Ivy, but it had been weeks since Ivy had been born, so the likelihood of nursing was low. Melissa's nurse had already thought about the situation and had talked with the charge nurse who gave the green light for Ivy to come for a brief visit. We would still need to wait a couple more days because Melissa was still very groggy, and we wanted her to be awake enough to enjoy the visit.

I was very excited about the prospect of Ivy's visit and couldn't wait to tell Ian. He was also very excited, and we started to make plans right away. We didn't tell Melissa that she would be getting a visitor because we didn't want her to be disappointed if things didn't work out. We were not completely sure that security would let Ian in with the baby, but the nurse had assured me that she would take care of that.

It was later decided that Ivy would come see Mommy on the 28th. By that time, Melissa should be able to be awake for longer periods of time, and there would be a better chance that she would remember her very first visit with her newborn.

Unfortunately, the coughing that had plagued Melissa was unrelenting, and had continued throughout the night, and into this morning. She would get very frustrated with the cough, because it also caused her discomfort. She was coughing so hard and so often that her ventilator tubing would fill with frothy red blood that the respiratory techs would frequently have to come in and drain. The doctors and nurses said that the cough and the blood was normal for COVID patients, but it was so hard to watch. Every time she leaned her head forward to cough, the trach would push out of the hole in her neck. The only reason that it didn't just pop right out was the strap that was clipped to either side. There were a couple of clean trach kits that the nurses kept on the windowsill of Melissa's room for emergencies. I was really hoping that they would never be used.

Even with the coughing, the ECMO tech turned the machine down even further. They lowered it to one, and then we had to wait two hours before checking her blood gas to make sure that her lungs were doing okay with the minimal support. They were, because the next time he came in, so did her doctor, nurse practitioner, and a couple of nurses. It scared me a little because it was not normal for all of them to come into her tiny room all at once, but I soon realized that it was nothing scary at all! In fact, it was a celebration, and everyone wanted to be in attendance because this time the tech turned the ECMO machine off.

Now the waiting started. Melissa would need to go twenty-four hours without the machine, and if she could, they would remove the tubes from her body.

Along with everyone celebrating the machine being turned off, we were also celebrating her last lung x-ray. Her previous x-rays looked like someone had stuffed her lungs with fluffy, white cotton. They had shown me a normal lung x-ray. I knew it should be almost completely black, except for a white haze where the heart sits, close to the spine, toward the bottom of the lung.

The x-ray tech brought his machine in today and took an x-ray. I was always required to stand outside the room, but I could still see the picture it took because it stayed on the screen of the machine. I was so excited about what I saw. There were still lots of white patches, but this time, her lungs were black with some white patches. Previous x-rays, her lungs were white with little to no black patches.

The x-ray was the most beautiful thing that I had ever seen, but I wanted the doctor to confirm that it was indeed much improved. He was in the hallway and allowed me to usher him into the room to look at the picture. He agreed it was a beautiful x-ray, and very significant to her recovery.

Recharged with all the good news, I sat down to write out a thank you text. I wanted to thank all the people who had prayed for Melissa, sent gifts and donated so generously to the GoFundMe that had been set up for Melissa and Ian by one of Ian's family members. Ian had no choice but to take a medical leave from work because Melissa had been the one to care for the girls while Ian went to work. Now, with Melissa in the hospital, Ian became the caretaker. They had been without income for several weeks now and there was no end in sight. Ian worked for a small company who could only give him a 30-day leave of absence, but that time had elapsed. He was now without a job altogether. Even when Melissa came home, she would not be able to care for herself, much less care for three small children. It astounded me how generous people, some who didn't even know us, had been. They received enough from the GoFundMe to keep the household going for a few months.

The wonderful apartment management worked hard to help them and made suggestions for State and Government-funded programs. We certainly live in a wonderful world, with truly kind, loving, and generous people.

As I hit send on my phone, I felt grateful to have had so many wonderful people who had touched our lives so profoundly.

"Hello everyone. I would like to start by thanking you for all the messages, texts, calls, donations, and prayers. We are overwhelmed by the care that everyone, including people we don't even know, who have prayed for Melissa, sent baby items, gifts for Harley, and have given so generously to Melissa and Ian's GoFundMe account."

"Melissa is doing amazingly well. She is no longer on sedation, but she still sleeps a lot. I tell her every day about all the people praying for her. I let her know that soon she will go home and wrap her arms around her children who miss her so much. This process has been a nightmare, but I will forever be grateful that I was given the opportunity to sit with my child while she recovered. Some did not get that opportunity."

"We hope they will take her off of the ECMO machine in the next several days and moved to a step-down unit. The doctors will then be able to wean her from the ventilator. We hope she will come home soon. I can't tell you how lucky we were that Melissa ended up in the hospital that she did. The skill and caring of the doctors, nurses, respiratory therapists, nursing assistants, and housekeeping are why Melissa is alive. Without them, we would live in a world that would forever be changed for us."

I truly felt that I had witnessed humanity at its best. Melissa had been placed in the path of skilled professionals whose determination to save her life was unending. We had been surrounded by thousands of people across the nation who had bowed their heads in prayer. A community of family, friends, medical professionals, and strangers had banded together to hold us up when we could not do it for ourselves. I will forever be grateful to each and every person who has touched our lives.

September 23, 2021

They turned the ECMO machine back on during the night. The doctor assured me that this was to be expected, and they would keep doing the trials with the machine off. Eventually Melissa's body would work without the support. It was disappointing, but they had warned that this would probably happen a few times before being able to take her off completely.

Zach was Melissa's nurse today. He had taken care of Melissa before, but only for a short time while her assigned nurse took a lunch break. I really didn't like it when we had a new nurse because it took a while to get used to them.

The minute I stepped into the room and took the hard folding chair off the wall, Zach stopped me. He said that he hated that chair and was sure I was tired of sitting in it. He asked me to hold on for a minute and he would be right back. When he came back, he was pushing a vinyl recliner through the doorway. I sank down into the chair, so happy to have something more comfortable to sit in. The very next time he walked back into the room, he was carrying a cup of hot, steamy coffee, which I accepted gratefully.

I texted my girlfriend, "Every day I come into the hospital, and I am disappointed that there is a new nurse. I'm afraid that I won't like them, but then I realize I was wrong, and they become my new favorite. Today Zack brought me a recliner and a nice hot cup of coffee."

My friend replied, "Sometimes, it's the smallest kindnesses that make us feel the best. Especially under your current circumstances."

My friend was right. Sometimes even the smallest act of kindness had an enormous impact and would be one thing that I would always remember.

September 24, 2021

The trials for being off of the ECMO continued on throughout the day. They would turn the machine off only to turn it back on after her next blood gas. It was frustrating. I just wanted to know for sure that her lungs could eventually make it with no support. The only way I was going to know for sure was if they could keep the machine off.

The doctor had reassured me that unless there was a serious infection or a blood clot, Melissa would recover and eventually go home. I had lived with the fear of Melissa dying for so long that it was really hard to feel totally comfortable. I would believe it once they removed her from the machine.

Melissa was still sleeping most of the time, which was no surprise. She was still on heavy pain medication, and her body was working overtime to heal. During the short periods of time that she was awake, I could see little glimpses of who she was before she got sick.

She has always had a sarcastic sense of humor and had always been very quick-witted. IVs, arterial lines, and other uncomfortable procedures were not always successful on the first try, and Melissa could see that it bothered the nurses when they had to try again. Even though those procedures were uncomfortable, she still managed to be funny and sarcastic with the nurses, even though she could not speak, and that made them feel better. It amazed me that my daughter was so resilient. It was wonderful to see that even in these circumstances, she could still display that same good humor.

Sometime around 2:00 p.m. the ECMO technician came in with good news. Melissa's blood gas was exactly where they wanted it to be, so he made a great big show of turning off the machine. We were all hoping that this was the last time they would ever turn the knob for Melissa. Several hours had passed and two blood gases drawn, but her levels remained where they should. When I left for the evening, the machine was still off.

Before going to sleep tonight, I made my nightly call to the hospital. When Melissa's nurse for the night shift came to the phone, he knew exactly what I wanted to know. The ECMO machine was still off, and Melissa's lungs were keeping up with the demands of her body.

Chapter Twelve

The Countdown

September 25, 2021

I knew that the night nurses were very busy, so I normally tried not to call more than once a night, but this time I couldn't help myself. I woke up two more times during the night and called to make sure that the machine had not been turned on again.

It was still off when I arrived this morning, and the countdown had begun. Seventeen hours had passed since they had turned it off, and she had six more to go. Everyone was excited, and we were all holding our breath.

Melissa was awake this morning, but I do not believe that she will remember anything from this time period because of the pain medication that was still necessary, although not in the same amounts as before. I was looking out the sliding glass door into the hallway in front of the nurse's desk. As I watched, a female patient walked a few steps across the hallway. She was connected to IV's and a ventilator that one nurse was pushing beside her. The woman could only walk three or four steps before having to sit down in the wheelchair that another nurse was pushing close behind her. They stood there for several minutes before taking three or four more steps.

It was at this time that I realized that this was the woman, Pamela, who had been weaned off of the ECMO machine, allowing Melissa to have this amazing chance at life. I was so grateful to see that she was doing well, but I had been told a few days ago that the doctors were not sure that they were going to be able to wean her from the ventilator.

Pamela was a little older than Melissa, but the situation was similar. She had contracted COVID while she was pregnant. Her baby had been born healthy, right before they put Pamela on the ventilator. Watching her struggle for breath as she took only three to four steps forced me to think about how much more road Melissa will have to travel. How much more hardship and suffering are still in her future, and that it would feel like forever before we will learn the extent of the permanent damage that COVID caused.

As they continued on their trip down the hall, I monitored the clock hanging above the door. It was now 1:30 p.m. and Melissa had only thirty more minutes to go before she reached her twenty-four-hour benchmark. The technician had already come in to draw the blood for the last blood gas test before her twenty-four-hour goal. It is so hard to wait.

When the ECMO tech walked back into the room, he spared me the anxiety of having to wait for him to speak. He was grinning from ear to ear as he walked to the whiteboard on the wall and wrote in great big letters, "24 hours off of ECMO!" The tubing was going to be removed from her body tomorrow. It was a moment of great joy, followed by great fear. What if they removed the tubing for the ECMO and then she needed it again? Would they have already put another patient on that machine, leaving Melissa with none?

The tech reassured me they knew at this point that Melissa was going to be okay without the machine. She would still need the ventilator, but that they would eventually start trying to wean her from that as well. I couldn't help but think back to Pamela, who I had seen struggling to walk down the hall and was afraid that getting off of the ventilator may not be as easy as they were making it sound.

September 26, 2021

We had a hard morning. I say we, because although it was hardest on Melissa, it took a great emotional toll on me as well. Melissa's bed was, once again, placed into a standing position. As her feet and legs bore some of her weight, she winced. I could see by the look on her face that standing was painful. Tears pooled in her eyes and escaped her lids to trickle down her cheeks. This time, we could not just push a button and let her sleep.

"Are you hurting, Melissa?" I asked. She could not advocate for herself, so I wanted to make sure that I did it for her if necessary. She nodded her head, confirming that she was feeling pain.

I asked questions about where she was hurting, but she could only mouth the words, "My knee." Melissa's face scrunched into a grimace.

As I spoke with the nurse caring for Melissa, to let her know she was having pain, I got the impression that I irritated her. She was very short when she answered. "I will lower the bed a little bit" and she did…a tiny amount. "But I'm not lowering it anymore." She said it as if I were being unreasonable, and then left, not only the room, but the floor.

By this time, Melissa was in genuine pain. She kept looking at me with tears streaming down her cheeks, mouthing the words, "My knee!"

She had no voice, and could not request the help that she needed, and I felt horrible for her. I didn't want to make the nurse angry, because I sure didn't want her to tell me to leave, but I could not allow Melissa to be abandoned and in pain. When I left the room in search of the nurse, she was nowhere to be found. I found another nurse, Zach, who had cared for Melissa before. When I told him that Melissa was in pain and crying, he came right away.

By the time we got back into her room, the ECMO technician was already at the door, and the bed representative followed in behind us. The three of us put our heads together to figure out a solution. Melissa had been flat on her back for weeks with her knees stick straight. I thought that if we could roll a towel up and place it under her knees so that they were slightly bent, she might be more comfortable. Zach and the technician both agreed that the towel would be a suitable solution even though her original nurse, who had since shown up, said that we couldn't possibly do what I had suggested. They rolled the towel up and placed it under Melissa's knees. With the problem solved, she completed the hour of standing.

As the representative for the bed company was leaving Melissa's room, he stopped at the threshold of the door, turned around to look at Melissa, and said cheerfully, "I'll see you later this afternoon!" I'm not sure what he was expecting. We were all very aware that Melissa didn't like him, or the torturous bed, but probably not expecting that she would roll her eyes at him. Even though she was well into adulthood, she still had that eye roll down to perfection!

The representative laughed a big, genuine laugh. "I love it that you feel well enough to roll your eyes at me; my job is done!" he boasted proudly. He laughed all the way down the hall, on his way to torture the next patient. It wasn't a celebratory moment for Melissa, but for those of us who knew where she had started, it was a wonderful moment. Melissa was slowly but surely returning to us.

September 27, 2021

They did not remove the tubing yesterday as expected because there was a new surgeon on duty, and he was not comfortable doing the procedure. He had not been at the hospital long and didn't want to take any risks with complications. He was still learning where all the equipment was, and if something went wrong, he would need to find things quickly.

Today's surgeon was happy to take the tubing out and was planning to do the procedure bedside instead of in the operating room. They asked me to leave the room and told me that they would come get me when it was done. While I waited, I spoke with the charge nurse to make final plans for Ivy's visit tomorrow. Ian and I are very excited to see Melissa's reaction when we bring her in. I think the nurses are just as excited.

It was at least forty-five minutes before the nurse came to get me. How wonderful it was to walk in and see that the tubing was gone and so was the machine. This was the first of the remaining two hurdles that were left for Melissa, and she did it! The next hurdle would be to wean off the ventilator. The doctors had already started the weaning process because Melissa was doing so well.

Melissa still needed constant reassurance that she was okay, which I was happy to give. She still couldn't speak, so even though she wanted to make conversation, she could not. Everything that she wanted to tell, or ask me, had to be communicated through pantomime, or the spelling sheet. If I sat down in the chair, I would have to stand up again in a couple of minutes, so I just stood beside her.

I don't really know what prompted me to lift the sheet other than I just had an overwhelming feeling that I should. When I lifted the sheet and looked at where the tubing had been in her groin, I saw the pool of blood that was bubbling out of the sutured wound and pooling beside her leg. I yelled for the nurse, Mike, who came right away. I didn't have to draw his attention to the blood because there was so much that he couldn't have missed it. He had come in with gloves on, so he immediately placed the heel of his hand on top of the wound and applied pressure. The doctor was called, and he asked that Mike continue the pressure for thirty minutes, and then he would decide if further intervention was necessary.

Her wound started bleeding as soon as Mike lifted his hands. They sent someone to get a device that would place continuous pressure on the wound so that Mike would no longer have to do it manually. The device was a clear plastic cup that looked something like a vice grip. The cup was positioned on top of the wound, and then cinched down tightly over her thigh, stopping the flow of blood. They left it on for forty minutes and then took it off.

Later that afternoon, when Mike came back in to move Melissa in the bed, her wound started to bleed again. Once more, he pressed his hands onto the bubbling wound and held pressure. His hands started to shake with the effort, but still he continued. Every once in a while, he would lift one hand and move his fingers around to relieve a cramp, but he never released the pressure.

The doctor asked for the plastic clamp to be placed back on, and mike complied, but not without requesting that a surgeon be called. He thought Melissa needed one more stitch to fully close the wound. When the surgeon looked, she felt everything was fine, but she had not seen how much blood Melissa had already lost. Melissa continued bleeding every time someone moved her, despite any of the measures taken.

Although I had been reassured by the nurse practitioner that Melissa was not in danger of bleeding to death because it was a vein and not an artery that was leaking, I was still worried. I was so relieved when Steve walked in for the night shift. As he came into the room, he exuded a confidence that was contagious. He had told me a few weeks ago that he would not allow anything within his control to happen to Melissa while he was there, and I believed him. He examined Melissa's sutures, sidled up to me, and with a wink, told me he would correct the issue as soon as the doctor left for the evening.

I left that evening knowing that Melissa was in excellent hands. Later that evening I received a text from Steve. It was a picture of Melissa, sitting up in a chair for the very first time! She had a little smile and looked like she may have been waving, but I wasn't sure. Steve had found that one stitch was loose, so he tightened it. Melissa was up and out of the bed with no bleeding.

September 28, 2021

Today was the big day that we had all been so excited about. Ivy was coming to meet Mommy! The nurse manager had let us know the day before that Ian could now visit. I would not have to bring Ivy by myself. I'm not really sure why they allowed both of us to come, unless they were just sick and tired of me being there, but I was glad whatever the reason. Ian had left early this morning so that he was there just as visiting hours started, but he did not tell Melissa about the visit. I stayed home to get Ivy dressed and ready to meet her Mommy. I felt bad that we could not take Harley, but the hospital would only allow Ivy to come.

When Ian got to Melissa's room, she was sitting in the recliner. I was happy to hear from Ian that Melissa was in fairly good spirits and had even managed a couple of laughs. Ian said that, although Melissa was enjoying his visit, he could tell that she was feeling frustrated with their inability to communicate. Melissa and I had practiced, so we were getting good at it. This was the first time for Ian and there was a big learning curve.

Unbeknownst to us, the doctor had scheduled Melissa for a CT scan this morning and they had neglected to let us know. Although Ivy and I were getting ready to come, we would have to wait until the transporters brought her back to the room. I knew that this was going to be a big energy drainer for Melissa, and it was disappointing to think that she may be too tired to enjoy Ivy's visit.

Once Melissa returned to her room, Ian gave the go ahead for us to head to the hospital. I loaded Ivy into her car seat and off we went. We waited in the family waiting room while the nurses got Melissa and her room, cleaned up, and ready for the visit. I followed Ian, who was holding Ivy, with my cell phone video going. The nurses had gathered in the hall in front of the room because everyone was excited to see the reunion. As Ian walked into the room holding Ivy, Melissa was falling asleep. She was so exhausted from her trip to CT that she could barely stay awake. Ian called Melissa's name, and she opened her eyes, but there was really no reaction at all. Ian placed Ivy on the bed next to Melissa and touched Ivy's hand to hers. Melissa moved her hand toward Ivy's, but then fell asleep again. The big, joyful reunion that we had all expected was not happening.

Ian and Ivy stayed for a few minutes before heading for home. The nurses said that Melissa's reaction was very normal, and that some moms were very joyful at seeing their newborn, but others were sad that they would not be going home to be with them. I'm not really sure that either was the case for

Melissa, because I found out later, they had given her some sedation for the CT scan, and that made it impossible for her to stay awake.

Later that afternoon, after Melissa had rested and was more awake, the speech therapist came in. She was holding a blue plastic case that contained a speaking valve. The valve fit over the top of the trach tube and allowed air to come into the valve, but did not allow air to flow out, forcing it up through the vocal cords, giving Melissa the ability to speak. Once the valve was secured onto the trach, the therapist asked, "Do you have anything that you would like to say?"

Melissa's speech was hesitant. Each word was separated by a long, drawn-out pause. "I … love … Ivy." I wanted to cry. I wasn't even sure if Melissa would remember that Ivy had been there, and I was so happy when she did.

September 29, 2021

Melissa is having such a hard time when I am not with her at the hospital. Last night, she picked up her cell phone. I had left it on her bedside table so that the nurses could help her FaceTime with me if she needed to. How she picked it up without dropping it is anyone's guess. I guess where there is a will, there is a way.

My phone rang just after midnight this morning. As I picked up the phone, I could see that the call was from Melissa's cell phone. I just about had a heart attack! "Honey, are you okay?" I don't know why I asked that because she couldn't speak. The only sound that I could hear was her tongue making the clicking noise, which was the only sound that she could make.

Click, click, click. Went her tongue.

I was panicking because I didn't know if something was wrong or if she just wanted me to talk to her. "Melissa, click once for yes, twice for no. Are you okay?"

Click. At least I knew she was okay.

"Do you need the nurse?"

Click. Yes, she needed the nurse.

"I am going to call the nurse. I will have her call me back from your phone so that I know she came in. Is that okay?"

Click.

"I love you," I said.

Click, click, click, click. I wasn't sure, but I hoped that meant that she loved me too.

I called the nurses' station to let them know Melissa had somehow called me on her phone, and I needed them to check on her. A few minutes later, the nurse called me back from Melissa's phone to let me know everything was fine.

As I drove to the hospital, I realized I needed to figure out a way for Melissa to safely pick her phone up. She still had very little control of her hands and fingers, and I really didn't understand how she had managed the call without dropping her phone. She just needed some kind of loop that attached to her phone so that she could stick her arm through it to lift the phone off of the table. Once the phone was over her lap, it would be better protected if it fell.

The nurse at the nurse's station was happy to give me a piece of copy paper and tape. I folded the paper over on itself several times, leaving one long strip. I taped both the inside and the outside of the paper, and then taped the two ends together, creating a stiff ring. Once I pried the case off of her phone, I set the paper ring inside the case, and then snapped the phone back into place. This created a ring that Melissa could stick her entire hand through, using more of her arm to lift the phone, than her hand and fingers.

I hoped that giving Melissa more power over her own body, as well as the ability to call me, or anyone that she wanted, might help reduce her anxiety when I could not be with her.

Wendy Reese

    She spent the next several hours looking through Facebook and reading text messages her best girlfriends had sent her, even when they knew she was on life support and may never see them.

Chapter Thirteen

Papa

September 30, 2021

Today was a big day for Melissa. They deemed her well enough to be moved from the ECMO ICU to a CCU floor on the other side of the hallway. Someone would still watch her all the time, but the nurse on this side of the floor would have two patients instead of one. We have been waiting for several hours because they were still getting the current patient transferred out to their new room and getting everything cleaned up and ready for Melissa.

    Melissa sat in the recliner in her room. To pass the time, she and I were using the spelling sheet to talk about little things. During a lull in the conversation, she clicked her tongue at me and brought my attention to the spelling sheet. As I watched the letters that she was pointing to, my heart fell. She had spelled out, "Papa."

    I tried to distract her, but she made a fist and softly pounded it on the paper, looking at me, expecting an answer. This really wasn't the right time to tell her. I didn't know if she would remember and that I might have to tell her again at a later time, but she was aware enough to ask. I was not going to lie. "Honey, Papa passed the other day." I really didn't know how to tell her, so I just said it. "He died at home, in his own bed, with Gran holding his hand." I told her that Dad, her aunt, and a few of her cousins had been there as he passed. I also told her that Papa had asked about her just a couple of days before he died.

Melissa sat there with silent tears streaming down her cheeks. I didn't know what to do or say, so I just kneeled on the floor and hugged her. After some time, she asked about Gran. She knew that this was going to be really hard on her. They had been married for so many years, and Gran had taken care of Papa for so long, as he had her, and his absence was going to be very hard for Gran.

We sat together quietly while Melissa absorbed the knowledge that Papa was gone. She asked how her dad was doing and wanted to know about funeral arrangements. Papa had not had a funeral because of COVID, but there had been a service for him at their church. It had been well attended, as Papa and Gran were well loved in their church and community.

Shortly after our conversation about Gran, Melissa moved down the hall to her new room. To prepare for rehab, physical therapy came in to work with Melissa. She could not do more than use her arms, and she could use her fingers somewhat, but only if she used them as a group and not individually. She would need to learn to sit up unassisted, stand, walk, and to take care of her basic needs. We were told that it would take months. The amount of care that she would need was overwhelming.

Timothy, the physical therapist, was young, high energy, and good looking. As he and his assistant walked in the door, he immediately began harassing Melissa. "M & M!" he exclaimed. "We gotta get you out of that bed!" Melissa's first, last, and middle name began with M, so M & M was the nickname that he chose for her. Timothy pulled her up into a sitting position, and his partner got on the bed behind Melissa, so that her body was leaning against his knees. She was not able to hold herself in a sitting position without support, but as hard as it was for her, she struggled through for several minutes before needing a rest. Timothy lay her back on the bed, but not before gently taking the ends of her dirty, messy hair in his hands and pulling it up and out on either side of her head. "Girl! You gotta do something about this hair! It's crazy!" He had a point. Her hair was a crazy mess.

    Melissa actually giggled at his teasing, which was unmerciful. She loved him and hoped that he would continue to work with her even after she went to the rehab. It was hard for her to think about having months of rehab before being able to go home. She wanted to be home with her family, in her own bed, with no nurses to wake her as soon as she fell asleep. Melissa was tired of having things done to her when she didn't want them to be done, and she felt voiceless, as if she had no autonomy. Even though I realized those things had to be done, I understood why she would feel that they were being forced on her.

    By this time, it was later in the evening, so I had only a little time to help her get settled before I had to go home for the night. It distressed Melissa that I had to leave. She had just moved to the new room and although it was just down the hall from her old room; it was all new nurses. I felt horrible having to leave her.

***

    I hated it when Mom went home tonight. Being in this new room, in a new unit, with all new nurses is scary. My mind is still foggy, and I'm only just now able to think clearly. I'm unable to sleep for more than a few hours at a time. I think it's because all the medications that I have been on are finally out of my system.

That only makes things more scary and incredibly lonely. I can't do anything for myself. I couldn't even push the call button if I needed to, so I'm left to my own devices until the nurse makes her rounds. I have asked the nurses to leave my door open during the night so that I can hear them walking by. Having the door open helps me feel a little safer and a little less alone.

I can't remember much before today. Mom filled me in on the last few weeks, but I can only remember little pieces of what happened. I have brief memories of Ian kissing me on my forehead, my mom patting my head and telling me I was okay, and just the faintest memory of Ivy visiting me. Other than that, my mind is blank. Most of my memories of the week before this nightmare began are gone as well. I remember being sick with COVID, visiting my OB to check on Ivy after office hours, being taken to the hospital by ambulance because I couldn't breathe, and then seeing Ivy's face the night that she was born.

Today was a day that I would rather forget. Papa is gone. It's hard to imagine that the strong, vibrant, loving, and gentle man that I grew up loving is no longer here. It's sad that he is gone, and that I wasn't able to see him one last time. I wish I could have been at his end-of-life service, and I can't imagine what Gran must be going through. Mom has told me that even while Gran is grieving, she still texts my mom for updates and to see how I'm doing. I don't know how she stays so strong and caring even in the worst times.

My name is Melissa, and I am the daughter in the bed.

***

Chapter Fourteen

Washing Hair

October 1, 2021

Melissa did not have the best of nights. She had spent the last 5 weeks sleeping, and now she could not sleep at all. I think she was afraid to go to sleep. I think she was afraid that she would slip back into that void of nothingness. I was sitting on her bed early this morning, and she was sitting in the recliner, when she leaned toward me, "Do you see the cockroach?" There was just a whisper of sound as she spoke. She had learned to speak around the trach, even though she should not have been able to. "What cockroach?" I asked. I had been in that hospital for weeks. I'm pretty sure that I would have noticed if there were roaches. Even so, I looked where she was looking. She was looking up at the ceiling directly over my head. There was a black spot on the ceiling tile, but it was just a stain. "Where is the roach, Melissa?"

Again, she mouthed the words, leaning toward me as if trying to keep it a secret from everyone else, "They are everywhere." She looked around the room like she could really see them, but there weren't any at all. I had been told that hallucinations were common with one of the sedation medications that she had been given, but I mentioned the conversation to her nurse Christie, just to be sure. She laughed and said that the guy in the room next to Melissa was seeing flying dragons. I'm not sure if dragons are better or worse than roaches.

I could tell that it irritated Melissa when I told her that the spot, she was seeing was only a stain and not a roach. She finally admitted that I was right about that particular spot, but she whispered under her breath that just because I was right about this spot, doesn't mean that there weren't cockroaches elsewhere.

Melissa really likes Christie, the morning nurse. They have just clicked, and I'm happy about that. I liked her too. She went above and beyond to make Melissa comfortable. When I asked if she could get me a few washcloths and a tub of water so that I could at least rinse some of the grease and blood out of Melissa's hair, she decided to do one better. There was a small sink in the front of Melissa's room, and she decided that if we could get the recliner over in front of it, I could wash her hair in the sink. She moved heaven and Earth to get Melissa over to that sink.

We moved the bed out of the room and into the hallway. Melissa was disconnected from the oxygen that was mounted on the wall and connected to a portable oxygen tank on wheels. The vinyl recliner, with her in it, was rolled in front of the sink. I was provided with several washcloths, shampoo, towels, a comb, and a waterproof mat that is usually used to prevent urine from soaking bed sheets but worked just as well for hair washing. We pushed the chair back, as flat as it would go, put the waterproof mat under Melissa's back and neck, and let it lay over the back of the chair and down into the sink. I had to wash Melissa's hair several times, but eventually, I got all the blood and grease out so that her hair was squeaky clean. After a good combing, I braided her hair in one long braid that hung neatly down her back. Melissa was excited for Timothy, the physical therapist, to see her newly cleaned and braided hair.

***

I was so happy to finally have clean hair! The realization that I had been in the same hospital bed for weeks made me feel so dirty and uncomfortable. I could feel how greasy my hair was and was glad that mom had offered to wash it for me. The actual washing of my hair felt great, however, the brushing was quite painful. I was not aware of it before but I'm finding parts of my body that aren't actually numb anymore but are now painful to touch. My scalp was one of them. I winced every time my mom ran the brush through my hair, but I sat there and took it because I wanted my hair to be clean so badly. Now Timothy will have nothing to tease me about!

I can't remember the nurses from the other unit that I had been on, but even if I could remember, I'm positive that Christie would still be my favorite. She was always so bubbly and did her best to communicate with me. Early this morning, before visiting hours, Christie was in my room doing some of her routine tasks and her back was to me. I had somehow managed to knock the ventilator tube off of my trach and although my mom had told me I had done that before and been fine, this time it made me panic. I was frantically trying to reconnect the tube, but I still had little control of my arms and hands. Christie turned around and saw my distress, so she came over and reconnected the tube. I was trying to compose myself and failing, so she put one hand on each of my shoulders and leaned in close to my face. She told me she was always watching my vitals, even from the nurse's station, and she promised she would always know if there was a problem with any of my equipment. She would let nothing bad happen to me. After I had calmed down some, Christie told me I didn't really need the ventilator, and that there were plans to take me off of it for a while later this morning. That made me feel relieved and excited. I would be one step closer to going home.

Christie is very thoughtful and is always looking for ways to help me be more independent. One of the more frustrating problems I was having was that I did not have the strength to push the call light button on my remote. It seems like such a minor task, but no matter how hard I tried, I just couldn't place enough pressure with my finger on the button. Christie came up with the idea to use a sticker that attaches a heart monitor to someone's chest. The sticker has a little silver button that the electrode would attach to, so she taped it upside down over the call light, which made it easier to push the button. That made me feel much safer, and more confident that I could call for help should I need it.

***

Chapter Fifteen

Outside

October 2, 2021

Melissa texted me this morning at 5:45 a.m. "Temmrrible right. Mmmnn. Yyhrt mmmmm" She was getting better with her fingers, but not enough for me to understand what she was trying to tell me.

I understood enough to know that she had said that she had a terrible night. "Sorry, honey. I will be in around nine. Are you okay?"

"Th report inhaler." She texted back.

"What?" I asked.

"Too miuvh. Call nurse."

She was asking me to call the nurse, so I did. Her nurse called me back a few minutes later to tell me that Melissa was fine and had just dropped her call light. I texted Melissa to let her know I would be there soon and told her I loved her.

"Love ♥and." Melissa texted back.

As I walked into Melissa's room later this morning, Christie and several other nurses had gathered in her room. Melissa was in her recliner, and she was on the portable oxygen tank.

Christie asked me, "Got any sunglasses? She's going to need them." Melissa had told Christie that she really wished she could go outside, so Christie was making her wish come true. They were going to wheel her down to the first floor, through the hall, and out to the flower garden.

The nurses pushed the chair out of the double doors that lead into the hall. I followed them out the doors and almost ran right into the cardiology doctor that I had met in the elevator several days ago. I had passed him in the hall every day since the elevator conversation, and he never failed to stop and ask about Melissa. Today, he got to meet her. He was already smiling when he saw her in the chair, but his smile got bigger when we told him she was going outside.

He stood in the doorway and watched as Melissa in her recliner, four nurses, one nurse practitioner, and one thrilled mom walked down the hall and out into the garden. We stayed there, letting Melissa sit in the shade, until sweat beaded on her forehead, and she decided she was tired and needed to go back in. It was a nice outing, and Melissa had thoroughly enjoyed it.

Shortly after getting back to her room, Melissa started coughing. The medication that they had given her to control it was wearing off. Every time she would cough, it pushed the feeding tube out of her nose, a little at a time. The nurses and I tried many times to retape the tube to the side of her cheek to keep it in place, but eventually, it dislodged enough that there was no choice but to remove it. Unfortunately, this meant that a new one would have to replace it. I waited with Melissa until visiting hours were over, but the team that places the feeding tubes never came. We assumed they would be by tomorrow since it was not urgent. I went home and to bed.

***

When Hope is Enough

Today was a day that I will always remember when I look back on my time in the hospital. While talking to Christie, I told her how much I missed being outside and how badly I wanted to feel the sun on my face. She told me that there may be a way we could make that happen, but she had to talk to some of the other nurses first. I was very hopeful and had hoped that we could make this happen just before mom came by so that she could come too. A little while later, Christie and four other nurses came in and got to work. They helped move me to the recliner, disconnect me from the machines in the room, and set up any of the portable machines that I would need to be connected to.

Once mom arrived, it was time to go! The nurses wheeled me out into the hallway and off we went. We paused a few rooms down so that we could say a quick hello to one of the other patients down the hall. I had only seen this man once before and I had heard bits and pieces about him and his family from my mom and the nurses. He was around my age and was a little further behind in his recovery than I was. I waved hello, and he waved back.

Mom had fallen a little behind because she had run into another doctor, so for a short time it was just the nurses and me. As we were moving through the hospital, down empty back hallways, Christie and the other two nurses started pushing my chair faster. Eventually, they were running through the halls, pushing my chair and sliding around corners as we all laughed.

We reached the doors that led out into the garden and as soon as we stepped outside, I felt the heat and humidity smack me in the face. It was overwhelming at first, although it is Florida, so I'm not sure what else I was expecting. The sun was bright and burned my eyes. Luckily, mom had brought a pair of sunglasses for me to use. We stayed outside for quite a while, just relaxing as I listened to the nurses and my mother talk to each other. A while later, I was sweaty and tired, so we decided it was time to go back to my room.

The rest of the day wasn't nearly as much fun. I had this terrible cough that medication could only control for a short while. I had been coughing so much lately that my feeding tube kept coming out a little each time. Once I finally stopped coughing, I had this awful taste in the back of my mouth, and I knew it was from my feeding tube. We had to remove the tube, and someone would replace it later in the day. I had hoped that my mom could be there, but eventually visiting hours were over and she had to go home.

***

October 3, 2021

***

"Took two hours, still no tube, so I refused it." Melissa texted at 5:45 a.m.

It was the middle of the night when my nurse and a few others entered my room. One of them was the tech who was going to place my new feeding tube. I knew the procedure would be unpleasant, but they had assured me that if everything went right, it would only take several minutes. Unfortunately, the tube kept getting kinked once it reached a certain point in my stomach, so the tech had to keep pulling the tube back and inserting again.

One nurse had brought a kit to work with all the supplies needed to paint her nails, and she asked me if that might help pass the time. I was happy for any distraction, so she grabbed the kit and let me pick from the colors she had. As that nurse was doing my nails, the other nurses and the tech were chatting about movies and music and other things.

When Hope is Enough

The subject of *The Lord of the Rings* series came up, and the tech mentioned she had never seen the movies. The other nurses were as surprised as I was! I could just imagine Ian's shocked gasp and proceeding lecture about how unacceptable that was.

At one point, the subject of hair color came up and one of my nurses, Christie, took her scrub cap off and showed off her purple hair. It surprised me because the doctors and nurses have always been so covered up that I never even imagined what hair color they had. I could only mouth words so I couldn't actually be part of the conversations, but I was happy to listen and hear about normal subjects for once. After two hours of countless tries, I decided I was done. I refused any more attempts and decided we could try again another time. Although, I secretly hope that I can take the swallow test before that happens and then I won't need a feeding tube anymore.

***

I was already up and getting ready to head to the hospital when Melissa texted me. When I arrived, she was not very happy. The team had come in early to place her new feeding tube but were never able to get the tube in the correct spot in her stomach.

The doctors had been talking about replacing Melissa's current trach with a smaller one because she could not use the speaking valve for more than two or three minutes at a time. She said that she felt like she couldn't breathe when the valve was on. Melissa and I hoped that once they put a smaller one in, she could use the speaking valve. Once she could use the valve, they would perform a swallow test, and then she would be allowed to eat and drink. Unfortunately, the pulmonologist decided she wanted to do a bronchoscopy before switching out the trach. Melissa was not happy because she knew nothing happens quickly in a hospital, and they would probably pressure her to allow them to try again to insert a new feeding tube. She really didn't want them to try again.

Although she was disappointed about the new trach being postponed, Melissa was thrilled that she had spent several hours without the ventilator. Instead of the oxygen tube being attached to her trach, they placed a small plastic cup that fit loosely in front of the trach tube in her neck. It did not push air into her lungs, but only directed warm, moist oxygen toward the trach, allowing her lungs to breathe with no mechanical assistance. It was much more comfortable than having the ventilator tube on. Because she had been doing so well, the doctors started talking about transferring her to a step-down unit, so when a room became available this afternoon, Melissa was transferred out of the CCU. This was a big step for her, and as soon as they cleared her to eat and drink, she would be ready to go to in-house rehab once a spot became available.

October 4, 2021

Melissa's new room was nice, but she was having a lot of anxiety. She did not have a dedicated nurse, or a nurse with just one patient, and she was left to her own devices for long periods of time.

Melissa sat in her bed flipping through the pictures of Ian, Alexandra, Harley, and Ivy. She looked happy. She said that she would really like to go home, but she understood that going to rehab was the best way to get her body back to normal.

Melissa had so hoped that she could nurse Ivy, and that hope was dwindling a little more with each passing day. When the unit secretary, also named Melissa, learned that Melissa wanted to nurse, she ordered a lactation consult and a breast pump. Melissa and I were so surprised when she brought it into the room. It was really very touching that she would go to that much trouble to help Melissa.

Melissa and I read the directions and figured out how to use the pump, even though I was very doubtful that it would work because so much time had elapsed since Ivy was delivered. She was somewhat successful, and it was only the first attempt.

This new room had a great big shower, and we hoped Melissa could take her first shower in six weeks, but that did not happen. A new room had opened on a different floor and Melissa was transferred for a second time today, to a new room. It was really great that she was doing so much better than anyone expected, but when she moved to her new room, she was all but forgotten. The nurses were so busy. They were trying their best, but since I was in the room with her, their attention went to other patients who were alone.

The bathroom in this new room is tiny, and there is no way that anyone could get Melissa into this shower with her mobility issues. She had worked with the occupational therapist this morning and had stood up with the help of a walker, but she could not pick her feet up and walk. She was able to shuffle her feet a little, so they brought in a bedside commode for her to use. It still required two nurses to assist Melissa to the commode, but Melissa preferred this to going in the bed and having to be cleaned up.

***

This was no fun at all! I really want something to drink, but they keep insisting that I wait. Every time I want to do something, I am asked to wait. I know the nurses are busy, but I am so uncomfortable.

The trach in my throat moves every time I swallow, try to talk, or move my head, and that throws me into a coughing fit. It is very hard to breathe with it and I have a hard time getting the mucus up from my lungs, so the nurses have to keep suctioning me. Being suctioned is awful! All the nurses have said that I need a smaller trach, like all the other ECMO patients, but the doctor insisted on doing a bronchoscopy before changing mine out. She did the procedure early this morning, but I feel like it was just a waste of time. I don't understand why my situation has to differ from everyone else's. I am trying so hard to be patient, but I am miserable and just want to go home and see my girls and Ian.

It's really hard to wait for the results to come back. I want a drink of Diet Coke so badly! My mouth always feels sticky, and it would feel great to actually take a drink. The speech therapist said that if the test results are okay, they will switch my trach and then send me for a swallow evaluation. I'm almost sure that I will pass, but there is enough doubt that it scares me a little. I will be so disappointed if they tell me I have to drink thickened liquids, or worse yet, nothing at all.

Mom and I killed some time playing cards while we waited for the speech therapist to come in with the results of the bronchoscopy. When the results came back a couple of hours later, although it felt like days to me, I was cleared for a smaller trach. The thought of them pulling my old trach out was a little scary. I did not know if it would hurt when they did it, but the fear was not enough to stop my excitement that having a smaller one would allow me to drink something.

The speech therapist said that she couldn't promise that they could replace my trach and get the swallow test done before my birthday on the eighth, but I really hoped that they could.

Not everything is horrible. Timothy zoomed by my room this morning on some kind of drivable patient lift. As he passed my door, he stuck his arm all the way out and pointed his finger at me. He was making a funny, scrunched-up face as he went by. He didn't just drive by my door and ignore me. He knew I was in this room, and he acknowledged me. It made me feel happy, and it made me feel like he cared about me. I know he cares about all of his patients as a group, but his acknowledgement made me feel like he also saw each of us as individuals.

***

Chapter Sixteen

Sleeping Meds and Strange Music

October 5, 2021

***

Last night was a particularly difficult night. Since the medications have worn off and I've become more aware, I have had a hard time sleeping. It didn't help that the patient in the next room was screaming day and night, calling for help. My nurse told me she wasn't in her right mind, and I felt sorry for her. At one point, I saw two officers rush past my door and had wondered what was going on. My nurse filled me in on the details when she came by to do her rounds. The officers were guarding an inmate who was here for treatment, and some of them came over to help with the screaming patient next to me. None of that really scared me, but the energy of this hospital floor made me feel more nervous and on edge.

As my nurse was administering my meds, she told me that my doctor had added a medication to help me sleep. After she left, I turned on the TV and tried to relax until the medication took effect. I could feel the medication kick in, but it didn't actually make me tired. Instead, I only felt more on edge. I had been watching some sort of musical called *Being for the Benefit of Mr. Kite*, which is actually pretty creepy when you're hopped up on sleeping meds. I tried to turn the channel, but I couldn't get my fingers to push hard enough on the buttons, so eventually I gave up and let the show play out. When it was over, the movie *ET* came on. I used to love that movie, but I don't think I'll ever be able to watch it again

***

 Melissa was very antsy today. She was feeling better and could move more easily both in the bed and in the recliner. Although she is still a two person transfer when the nurses move her to the bed or into the chair, she can help some. She can shuffle her feet to turn in a circle, but to be safe, they always have two people to assist because she is still off balance.
 When I asked her why she was so antsy, she told me about an incident that she had last night with a nurse. He did not understand her needs and did not listen when she tried to explain those needs to him. I won't go into detail, but he left her in a very uncomfortable position that was totally avoidable if he had only listened. The entire situation could have been prevented if they would have allowed me to stay the night with her.
 We spoke with the shift charge nurse, and they gave me permission to stay with Melissa for the night.

October 6, 2021

 Melissa and I woke up very early this morning. It's impossible to sleep much in a hospital because nurses and CNAs come in every couple of hours to check vitals and to give medication, but that didn't really matter. Melissa could not sleep even if they had left her without the interruption. That meant that I had not slept either. We were both a little grumpy, and we both wanted to go home.

I didn't want to be at the hospital anymore, and neither did Melissa. We wanted things to go back to normal. It's not that I didn't want to be at the hospital with Melissa. I just wanted things to go back to how they were before she got sick. Normal was sitting on my couch watching *Ghost Hunters* or *Pitbull's and Parolees* with Emily. Normal was sitting in bed talking with my husband. Normal was knowing that Melissa was at home with her children and not having ever suffered this horrible illness. Normal was me not having to know what it felt like to almost lose my child. Normal was permanently changed for us and we would have to adjust.

Melissa was sitting in the recliner later this morning when Timothy walked in. She was happy to see him, but I think it made her feel bad when he asked why she was sitting around instead of walking. Melissa had begged the nurses to let her walk. She wanted to get out of that hospital as soon as possible, and walking was the fastest way to achieve that goal. She told Timothy that she had asked repeatedly if the nurses would allow me to walk with her, but she was told no.

***

After being moved twice and each floor being worse than the last one, I was fed up. I'm glad that I seem to be doing better than any of the doctors expected, but the rooms I kept moving to were nothing but a disappointment. The first room had a big bathroom with a shower, and I was desperately hoping that I could finally take a shower but my nurse and the others on the floor were so busy that she couldn't bring in the help she needed to move me into the bathroom.

My nurse was nice enough, but now that I was on a floor where each nurse had several patients, I only saw her when I absolutely needed something or when it was time for my medications.

The second room was even worse than the previous one. The bathroom was so tiny that there was no way that I could get into the shower. My nurses on this floor are different every shift.

The biggest frustration, though, was having to wait for my procedure before sizing down my trach. I thought it was ridiculous that my speech therapist had said my case was the same as some of her previous ones and that my trach just needed to be sized down, but my doctor thought this procedure was necessary. That meant that I would have to have my feeding tube re-placed, and that I was that much further from being able to move to the rehab floor.

I felt trapped. My doctors were so happy with my progress and how I was recovering, but then each time I feel ready to take the next step, I'm being told to wait or slow down. I can't slow down. I don't even remember spending time with Ivy after she was born and while everyone is home fawning over my baby; I am here, in this bed. I haven't seen Ian, Alex, or Harley, and I just want to go home. I want to be able to eat and sleep and be with my family. The thought of being stuck here is really starting to make me panic, and my poor mother is the one who has to deal with me.

After the procedure, my mom and I killed time playing cards while waiting for the results. It seemed like an eternity when the speech therapist came back with the results of the bronchoscopy. I was cleared for a smaller trach, and the speech therapist would schedule the procedure, as well as the swallow test, as soon as possible. There was no guarantee that it would happen before my birthday which was in four days. That was disappointing. I had been so hopeful that I would be able to eat on my birthday and finally have a Diet Coke. I will just have to wait until I can take the swallow test and pray that I will be cleared for all foods and liquids.

***

    We knew how busy the nurses were. We certainly didn't blame them for being so busy, but that didn't change the fact that Melissa needed to get up and move to get better. Timothy said that he would speak with the nurses about allowing me to walk with her, but first he wanted to get her up and walking. He assisted Melissa to a standing position and then handed her a walker. She had to rock back and forth on the bed to get enough momentum to stand up. We had to watch that she didn't rock so far forward that she would just keep going as she stood. We certainly didn't want her to end up on the floor.

    She slowly shuffled her way to the door where a wheelchair sat waiting for her. I followed along closely with the wheelchair while Timothy walked next to her with the heart monitor. Melissa made it halfway down the hall before Timothy asked her to rest and allow her heart rate to slow down. It amazed me how far she had made it on her very first walk. Timothy was impressed with how well Melissa was doing. He had not expected her to walk more than a few steps at a time, but she was determined to get stronger so that she could go home.

    While Melissa rested in the wheelchair, she told Timothy about going outside when she was in the CCU. She told him how happy it had made her feel to sit in the sun, away from everything that reminded her of the hospital. He asked her why she hadn't been out again, and Melissa explained the nurses didn't have the time to take her. Timothy asked us to wait where we were and said that he would be right back. When he returned, he asked me to get Melissa some sunglasses because he had gotten permission from her doctor to take her outside.

Timothy understood that as important as it was for Melissa to use her muscles, it was just as important for her to have those little moments. She needed to feel as normal as possible. While Melissa sat basking in the sun, Timothy asked about her children. When he learned that she had not seen her kids for the entire six weeks he was upset for her. He was a father of two, and he could relate to how hard it must be for her, and for the girls, to have not seen them for so long.

When Melissa mentioned that her twenty-eighth birthday was only two days from today, he decided he would arrange a family visit as his birthday gift to her. He set the time for 11:00 a.m. on the eighth. While we slowly strolled back to Melissa's room, she chatted happily away. She was so excited! She talked about seeing the girls for the rest of the day. I was glad that she had something fun to look forward to instead of spending her birthday alone in the hospital.

October 7, 2021

Melissa is no longer on the ventilator, nor does she need the cup that moistens the air for her. She is breathing completely on her own, and she has surprised everyone with how quickly she transitioned to room air. Now she could move to the rehab center because she no longer needed the ventilator or the feeding tube. They were working on getting her a room and would let us know as soon as one became available.

Since Melissa no longer had to be connected to IVs or oxygen, it is much easier for her to move around. Timothy had spoken with Melissa's doctor. She had given permission for me to take Melissa into the hallway and let her walk, as long as I followed closely with the wheelchair and monitored her heart rate. Melissa took full advantage of her ability to walk, and we went for a stroll around the nurse's station several times in the next couple of hours.

We were out in the hall when one of the pulmonary doctors walked into the unit. She asked us to return to the room because they were going to change Melissa's trach to a smaller one. It was kind of funny to see how quickly Melissa moved when there was motivation.

The pulmonary doctor asked Melissa to lie back on the bed and tilt her chin up toward the ceiling. Melissa's hands shook a little. She asked the doctor how long it took to switch the trach. The doctor said that they just pull the old one out and stick the new one in. I am sure she was afraid that it was going to hurt. She said "ouch" when the old one popped out of the hole in her neck, but it happened so quickly that there really wasn't time for her to feel much.

As soon as the doctor inserted the new, smaller trach, Melissa cried. The pulmonary doctor asked if she was okay, but Melissa wasn't crying because she hurt. She was crying because the smaller trach was drastically more comfortable, and it was so much easier for her to breathe. I had not realized how uncomfortable the old trach limited her ability to breathe until I saw her reaction to the new one.

I had never realized that breathing through the trach felt like breathing through a straw. Melissa had to work much harder to get a breath, and it was a very claustrophobic feeling for her to have to work so hard. This new, smaller trach didn't take up as much room inside her trachea. She could breathe through and around it, and it wasn't as long as the old one, so it did not tickle her throat and make her cough every time she moved her head.

***

Wendy Reese

I was nervous when it came time to change my trach for a smaller one. I knew I didn't NEED it to breathe, but it still scared me that something may go wrong or that it would hurt. Surprisingly, it took maybe a minute to change my trach to the smaller size, and it only really hurt when they pulled it out, but that pain subsided quickly.

Once they got the new smaller trach in place and I took a breath, it was like night and day. I didn't even truly realize how challenging the old trach had been to breathe with until I felt what it was like to breathe with this smaller one. I also didn't feel that awful urge to cough anymore.

The biggest surprise, though, was that I could now talk. I could actually get out full sentences and still be able to breathe at the same time! This rush of relief came over me and I started to cry. One more hurdle jumped. One step closer to leaving!

***

The next hurdle will be for Melissa to pass the swallow test, and if she does, she will be allowed to eat and drink. Melissa has not had a single sip or bite of anything for the last seven weeks. She wants a Diet Coke so badly and had been talking about it for days. When the transporter came to take Melissa for her test, I went to the gift shop to get her the soda, and some flowers for her birthday. I was sure that she was going to pass the test, and I wanted her to have the drink immediately. As soon as I came back to the room, I set out the birthday decorations that I had purchased the day before. It was a day early, but I wanted her to enjoy them for a while.

When she returned to the room, they had given her the green light to eat or drink anything that she desired. It was wonderful watching her take that very first sip of soda. We ordered her first dinner of grilled cheese and apple sauce to be delivered later in the evening.

***

When Hope is Enough

When I arrived back from my swallow test, I was excited to let mom know I had passed and was cleared to eat and drink anything I wanted.

As they wheeled me up to the room, I saw some decorations hanging in the doorway. Mom had decorated the room for my birthday a day early so that I could enjoy the decorations longer.

There was also a Diet Coke waiting for me! I was so excited to take that first sip, but when I felt that first sip hit my tongue, it was awful! The bubbly feeling was wonderful, but it tasted awful. COVID had definitely affected my taste buds. Now I'm worried that my first meal is going to taste just as awful. At least I can eat as many ice chips as I want!

***

Soon after ordering the food, the occupational therapist showed up. Timothy had arranged for her to take Melissa up to the rehab floor and to help her take her very first shower in ten weeks. When we entered the shower room, the therapist assisted Melissa to a shower chair. After warning her not to face the stream of water directly so that the water would not get inside her trach, she closed the plastic curtain, allowing Melissa some privacy. She spent the next fifteen minutes sitting on the bench, just enjoying the feeling of the hot water raining down on her.

Melissa said that the shower felt wonderful as the stream of hot water washed the remaining dried blood and grease from the back of her hair and down the drain. It was as if she was washing the horror of the past weeks away. She felt a great sense of freedom. It felt nice being allowed to sit on the bench by herself and decide how long her shower would be, instead of having it done for her quickly. Melissa went to bed feeling very clean and very excited for the next day.

Chapter Seventeen

Visiting Day

October 8, 2021

Melissa was still having trouble sleeping. She was afraid to sleep but could not tell me why. After what she had been through, I really couldn't blame her. To pass the time, and to help me stay awake, we played cards and colored in her coloring book. I had purchased both the cards and the coloring books a few days ago, thinking that it would be a fun way for her to stay busy, but would also help develop her fine motor skills and finger strength.

As the eleven o'clock hour approached, I dressed Melissa in a new red and white striped nightgown I had given her for her birthday and brushed and braided her hair. She looked beautiful, and she was glowing for the first time in weeks.

Timothy walked into her room about fifteen minutes early. He helped Melissa transfer over to the wheelchair, and we all headed out to the front of the hospital. Just outside the front doors of the hospital, there is a little cafeteria for hospital staff and visitors, and that is where we were meeting Ian and the girls. As we wheeled Melissa out the door, she got her first glimpse of her family.

Ian was carrying a large vase of red roses. Alexandra's hands were full trying to keep control of several Mylar balloons that the wind was trying to steal. Harley followed closely behind with a beautifully decorated chocolate cupcake, which she was carrying carefully in her cupped hands.

Both girls hurried toward the wheelchair but stopped before getting too close. They stood there awkwardly, looking at Melissa until I realized they were afraid to touch Mommy because they didn't want to hurt her. Once Melissa told them they would not hurt her and asked for hugs, the girls were all over her.

Once the hugs were done, we settled Melissa by one of the black bistro tables. Ian asked if she would like to hold Ivy. Of course she did, so she held her arms out for Ian to place Ivy in her arms. She still needed help to support Ivy's weight, but Alexandra was happy to help.

I sat at the table across from her, watching the girls hang on her like they never wanted to let her go. We had been in crisis mode for so long. We had lived for over a month, not knowing if Melissa was going to live or die, and it was hard for my mind to accept that it was over. It was hard for my mind to stop thinking back on the horrible things that I had witnessed and the abject fear that I felt, thinking that I might lose my child. I think fear like that imprints on your mind, and it never leaves. I think it breaks you a little and can't be repaired.

***

I was so happy to see Ian and the girls for the first time today. It felt like a lifetime had passed since I had seen them, and Ivy was so big despite only being 6 weeks old. After returning to my room, I felt a rush of sadness. I knew that the visit was meant to be a happy moment and make me feel better, but I now just felt sad and a little resentful that they all got to go back home, and I was stuck in this hospital bed.

***

Alexandra's Worries

Today was a really happy day. We got to go to the hospital to see mommy! Ian let me carry the balloons we were bringing for Mommy's birthday. I thought we would go to Mommy's room, and she would be hooked up to all the machines, but when we saw Mommy, she was in a wheelchair outside the hospital. I helped Mommy hold Ivy because Ivy is heavy, and Mommy is not very strong because of the machine she had been on. It was a good day, but Ian, Harley, and I were sad when we had to leave Mommy at the hospital. We were afraid she was sad when we left.

Chapter Eighteen

Going Home

October 9, 2021

Melissa spent the morning thinking that she was going to be headed off to rehab in the next day or two. Although she didn't want to go, she had been told that it was the best thing for her. She told me she really wanted to go home and touch little baby feet. It was hard for her to know that it would be several more weeks before she could do that. She was understandably upset when the caseworker came in and told her it might be another week or two before there was an open spot for her.

Melissa decided at that moment that she was done and was going to go home. She had been willing to go to rehab so that she could regain her strength. Now she felt she would waste an entire week or two sitting in that hospital room when she could be home with her family. The doctors warned her she should not leave without rehab. The physical therapist told her he thought she would be beyond needing rehab if she had to wait much longer.

The hospital agreed to discharge her as soon as they could make sure that she had the equipment that she needed. Everyone agreed Melissa would be safe going home, but the doctors and the physical therapist had differing opinions about the rehab. There was a lot of back and forth, and a little of arguing from me, but eventually they got everything in place for Melissa to go home. She would go home with the trach still in place and would have to have it removed in the doctor's office in the next several days.

I packed everything that she had accumulated at the hospital and placed it on the rolling cart they provided. We waited several hours for the discharge paperwork to be done and it was nearing nine o'clock when the hospital officially discharged Melissa. As I drove my SUV up to the patient loading area, a nurse wheeled Melissa out of the hospital doors for the last time and assisted her into the car. I placed her possessions in the back seat.

It was the strangest feeling to be driving away from the hospital with Melissa in the seat next to me, knowing that we would not be coming back. It felt like our departure was too simple and too quiet. This was such a momentous occasion, and it felt like there should be trumpets and fireworks, but of course there wasn't. We just calmly drove away into the night.

That little voice that had whispered in my head, telling me that everything was going to be okay, had been right. It was over and Melissa had survived.

Melissa was going to come home with me to my home where there were no apartment stairs. I had the time to dedicate to helping her with rehab and taking her to doctor appointments. Ian could not care for the girls and Melissa at the same time. How could he get Melissa and the girls downstairs and into the car when Melissa had appointments?

Melissa wanted to spend the night at her apartment with Ian and the girls and then we would leave for my home in the morning. Unfortunately, Harley started to run a fever the night before and had cold-like symptoms, so it was not safe to expose Melissa.

She was so disappointed and wanted to see them so badly that we drove to the apartment; Melissa would stay in the car. Ian and the girls could come outside and talk to her through the car window. It was the best that we could do and still keep Melissa safe. They had warned Melissa that her lungs would not survive another respiratory illness.

Alexandra's Worries

Ian said that Mommy was leaving the hospital, but she wasn't coming home. He said that Harley was sick, and we couldn't take any chances that she would get sick again. Grammy came to the apartment to get some of Mommy's clothes, but Mommy stayed in the car. We went downstairs and into the parking lot and talked to her through the car window. We couldn't get very close, and we weren't able to hug her. I was proud that Ian let me carry Ivy out to the car and show her to Mommy. I was really careful not to trip, and I held her tight because I didn't want to drop her.

We arrived at my house at one o'clock in the morning. Melissa's sister and my husband came out to help get Melissa inside and settled in. We had the suction machine and a walker, but Melissa refused to use the walker, insisting on walking from the car, through the garage, and into the house by herself. I was really worried that she would fall and annoyingly followed right behind her with my arms out on either side to catch her if she fell, but she didn't. She went slowly, but she was very steady and determined.

We woke up this morning, and with a lot of trial and error, did her first round of trach care. It involved removing the pad from around the trach, cleaning it, and then replacing the pad. I was very awkward, and it took me much longer to finish than it did the nurses at the hospital, but Melissa was very patient with me.

By the end of the day, Melissa's neck was feeling sore. We worried she may be getting an infection at her tracheostomy site, so we headed to the local ER the next morning.

We had made an appointment with the pulmonary doctor that the hospital had recommended to remove her trach, but they could not get her in for two months. We hoped they could take the trach out since she no longer needed it, but unfortunately, they were not comfortable taking it out. They did not have the respiratory support and suggested that we go back to the ER department of the Orlando Hospital.

We drove the two hours to Orlando and checked in at the reception desk of the ER. When I gave Melissa's name, the receptionist knew who Melissa was. All the ER staff knew who she was, and they were all so happy and willing to help. Apparently, Melissa was a celebrity at the hospital, and the entire staff knew her story.

The ER doctor, after confirming with the pulmonary doctor, was happy to take the trach out. He asked Melissa to sit back on the bed and tilt her head backwards just a little. After removing the neck strap from the clip on the trach, he pulled out and down. The trach came right out.

The hole in the skin of her neck stayed open a little and I could hear the air push out through the wound when she would breathe out. It got much louder as she spoke. Her voice sounded breathy and a little horse, but the doctor said that was normal and that the windpipe would eventually heal, and the skin would close on its own.

They had us sit there for an hour just to make sure that she did not have any difficulty with breathing. When the hour was up, they sent us home.

We were so close to Melissa's apartment, and she wanted to stop by and see Ian and the girls. She missed them so much and really wanted to opportunity to know this new child that she had brought into the world.

Ian met us at the door as I pushed the wheelchair, with Melissa in it, over the threshold. I hadn't even pushed her all the way into the apartment and was still standing outside the door, but Ian didn't wait. He bent down and wrapped his arms around Melissa's waist, lifting her from her seat and just held her tightly. He stood there for a long time, just holding her. I knew at that moment that Melissa was probably not going to be coming back home with me.

When it was time to leave the next morning, sure enough, Melissa told me she was not coming back home with me. She wanted to stay home with Ian and the girls. I understood how she felt, but I was worried that Ian could not provide the care that Melissa would need while taking care of a three-year-old and a newborn. They were on the second story of an apartment building. What if the apartment caught fire? How would Ian get the baby, Harley, and Melissa out safely? When I posed this question to Melissa, she said that she would crawl down the stairs while Ian carried the girls. I did not agree with the decision, but I eventually relented.

I worried all the way home and for the next several days. I called Melissa more often than she probably wanted me to, but it was impossible for my brain to just stop being in crisis mode. For six weeks, I didn't know if Melissa would ever come home, and now that she was home, I didn't know how to make my brain stop worrying. I didn't know how to make my heart stop missing a beat and for the anxiety to stop rising in my chest when I would relax, and my mind would wander back to the hospital where it was used to being. I didn't know how to stop the tears that would escape from my eyelids in those moments when I forgot it was over and that Melissa had survived.

An entire week passed before I could drive back to Orlando to check up on Melissa, Ian, and the girls. When I walked into the apartment, Melissa was sitting on the couch folding dish towels. Ian had tasked her with that household chore because she could do it. It was difficult, and it took her a while, but she could do it.

As I walked toward her to give her a hug, she tried to stand. I hurried forward to assist her, but she put her hand out to stop my forward movement. "I can do it Mom.! It took her several tries, but she did indeed do it on her own. She had told me a day ago that Ian had taken her to CVS because she needed to pick up a prescription. It impressed me when she told me she had walked all the way down the hall, into the elevator, and out to the parking lot. She walked into the pharmacy instead of using the wheelchair and then reversed the process to get home.

At this moment, the realization hit me. I had been wrong. Ian could absolutely take care of her and the girls. In fact, he may help her more than I could. As hard as I tried not to, it was instinct to remove any obstacle that I could from her path, but her need for that was over. I had done my job and now it was Ian's turn. I wanted to make things easy for her. What she really needed was someone who treated her like a partner and not someone who was incapable of completing simple tasks on her own. Ian was that person.

My part in Melissa's recovery was done. It was now time for Melissa and Ian to work together. Melissa would have to work hard to become her pre-COVID self. Ian would need patience and persistence to help Melissa with the emotional side of recovery as well as the physical. I left knowing that they are both very capable of dealing with what was next. They would find their new path and would traverse it well.

When Hope is Enough

As I drove home, I spent the entire two-hour drive thinking about how lucky I was. How fortunate our family was that Melissa had lived, that Ivy was healthy, and that Melissa had the opportunity to continue her life path.

I thought about how grateful I was for the gift that the universe had given me when my husband Donny came into my life. During this entire ordeal, my husband was there. He stayed quietly in the background, making sure that the only thing I had to worry about was the one thing that he could not lift from my shoulders. He took the worry about the household chores, my youngest daughter, the pets, the financial aspect, all of it, away from me and had allowed me to worry only about Melissa. He took away the guilt I felt for being gone for six weeks. He was always there for reassurance, and he never told me how I should feel or what I should think. He was just always there. I will forever be grateful for this man that I am married to.

Epilogue

Melissa continued to recover and with Ian's help, she regained most of her strength.

Life continued on, but it did not go back to normal. Nothing would ever be normal again. I now knew what it felt like to sit by my child's bed, hold her hand, and wait for her to die. I would never be able to forget the all-encompassing devastation that came with that knowledge.

I left little pieces of my heart in the rooms and hallways of that hospital. Those pieces intertwined with pieces left from previous patients echoing through the hospital, some joyful with recovery and others grief-stricken with loss. My heart felt like it would never be whole again, and I felt broken. Maybe that is how I was supposed to feel.

Maybe I was supposed to learn something from this experience. The lesson that I took was that we don't know how much time any of us have. We should use the time that we have on this Earth, doing all the things that we plan on doing later….when the time is right….when we have the money…..when, when, when. I say we should do those things now. We should make those memories that we might miss out on if we wait for a perfect time. Right now, is the perfect time!

Love your family and friends like today is your last day, because you never know. It may be.

When Hope is Enough
February 19, 2022

It was a beautiful, warm evening in Central Florida. White folding chairs sat lined up on the lawn, leaving a space big enough for two people to walk down side by side.

Emily, Melissa's little sister, walked down the aisle and took her seat. My husband followed her, holding Ivy. Alex and her two cousins walked down the aisle toward us and stood to the right of the archway. Harley refused to walk at all, so Nona picked her up and carried her to the front row and sat down, holding her in her lap.

I stood at the end of the aisle with Ian while the guests turned to watch the beautiful bride walk down the aisle on the arm of her father. As they reached the end of the aisle, Ian stepped forward, shook Eric's hand, and then Melissa and Ian turned to face me. It was an honor for me to perform the ceremony that would join Melissa and Ian as husband and wife.

I began by welcoming the guests and thanking them for being with us on such a special day.

The ceremony concluded, and Ian kissed his bride

As the guests stood up to cheer, Melissa and Ian walked back down the aisle holding hands; Melissa's adorned with her new silver wedding band, and Ian's, a black band with a silver Batman sign engraved on it. The warm breeze gently blew across my skin as the sun lowered its position on the horizon, the clouds turning a beautiful purple and pink in the otherwise clear sky. I watched the bride and groom walk away from me to their new life, a life just waiting for them, so full of promise, and I felt happy. I was no longer the mother in the chair, and she was not the daughter in the bed. I was just mom, and she was my daughter.

Hope had been enough. Hope had won.

In Loving Memory of
William "Buddy" Terrell

I thought of you with love today but that is nothing new. I thought about you yesterday and days before that too. I think of you in silence. I often speak your name. All I have are memories and your picture in a frame. Your memory is my keepsake with which I'll never part. God has you in His keeping. I have you in my heart.

Written by Unknown Author

When Hope is Enough

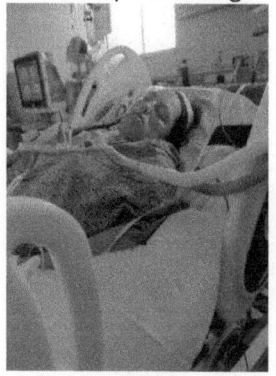
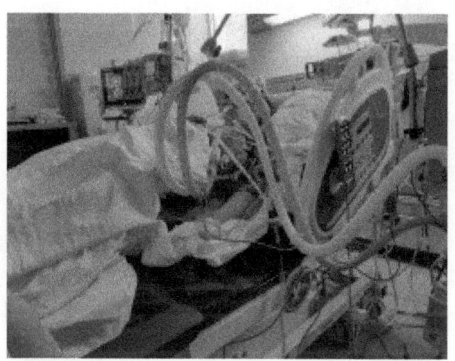
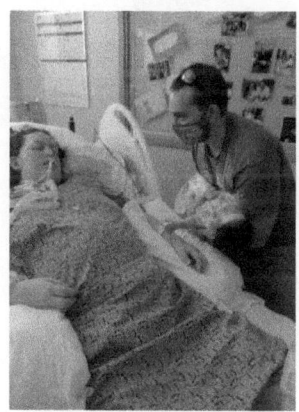
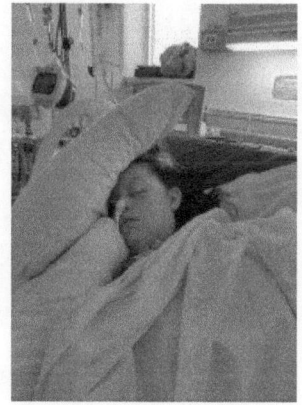

Wendy Reese

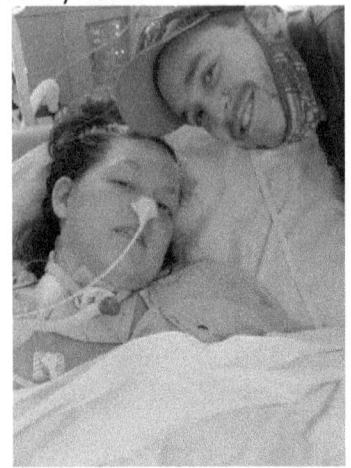
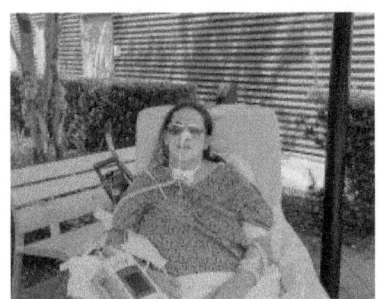

Dear Readers,

Thank you for allowing me to share this journey with you.

If you enjoyed reading this story, please take a short moment to write a review on Amazon.

If you have any comments or experiences that you would like to share, please email me at wendywritesbooks@gmail.com.

I would love to hear from you.

Sincerely,

Melissa's Mom, Wendy

Wendy Reese

There are so many people who I am thankful for. If I did not directly mention you, please know that you have not been forgotten. I will forever be grateful for everyone that touched us in thought, prayer, hope, or in life during this time.

My wonderful husband, Donny. Thank you for allowing me to be with Melissa during this awful time without having to worry about anything else. Your reassuring presence was constant, and I will forever be grateful that you are my husband. Thank you for encouraging me to write this book even during the many hours that I ignored you while doing so. I appreciated your thoughts and ideas for the story, and I could not have written it without you.

Mom, thank you for answering the phone every single time that I called. Thank you for being with me on the phone every night as I left the hospital and walked through the dark parking garage, once again looking for my car. I always knew that you were just a phone call away and even though I am 56 years old, I still need my mom.

Jina, my dear friend. Thank you for your unwavering support during Melissa's hospitalization and throughout our friendship. You will never know how much those daily calls and texts brought me back down to reality when panic was so easy to give in to. Thank you for reading draft after draft and making valuable suggestions. You are the best friend anyone could ask for.

Emily, thank you for understanding why I could not be with you while you were dealing with Melissa's illness but also suffering the loss of someone that I know you loved so much.

Christy and Laurie, thank you for being there for me. Thank you for allowing me to tell this story over and over until it didn't hurt so much.

Scott, you were my hero that day in the parking garage. I don't know what would have happened if you had not intervened. Thank you for all the times that you brought me back down with your calm reassurance.

Kellie, thank you for being the first person to read the entire book and give me feedback. I loved your ideas and suggestions, and I am so glad we are friends!

Thank you to Joe and Laura for listening to me during the times I took a lunch break. I could not stand to sit alone and listen to the voices in my head. Thank you for keeping me company.

Most of all, thank you to ORMC and all of its staff for keeping my daughter alive. The skill and care that was shown to us was extraordinary. Without all of you, my world, and the world for Ian, Alexandra, Harley, and Ivy, would be irrevocably changed.

When Hope is Enough

Lightning Source UK Ltd.
Milton Keynes UK
UKHW010114100123
415068UK00007B/755